SHEET PAN

delicious recipes for hands-off meals

KATE McMILLAN

Photography by
RAY KACHATORIAN

weldon**owen**

CONTENTS

easy & delicious one-pan meals **10**

sheet-pan basics **15**

meat **19**

seafood **63**

vegetables **85**

index **108**

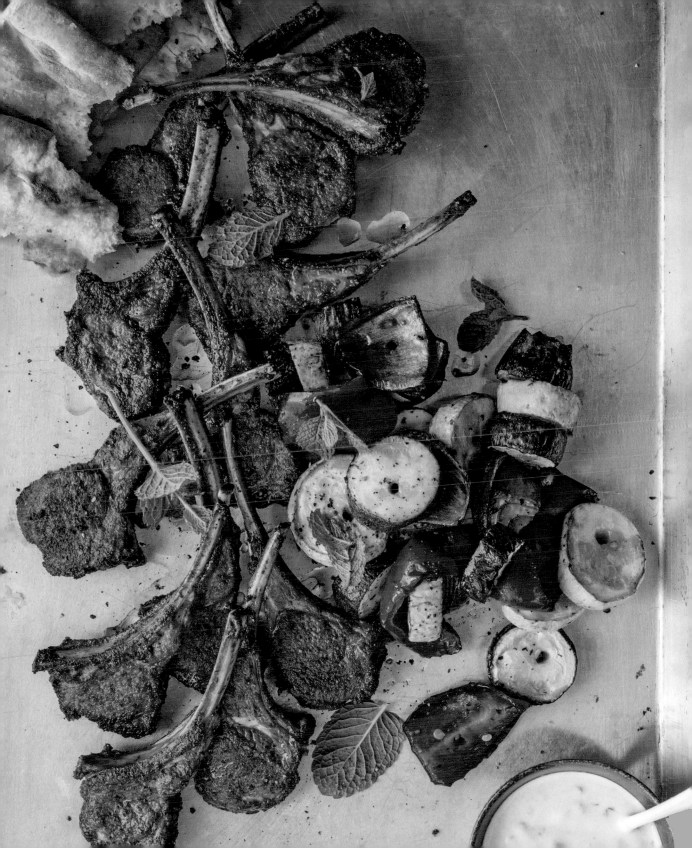

EASY & DELICIOUS ONE-PAN MEALS

Sometimes the simplest way is also the best way, which is the idea behind this book: sheet-pan cooking is not only easy, it's also a remarkably effective—and versatile— way to prepare one-pan meals. Offering the same kind of simplicity and convenience as one-pot cooking, sheet pans are especially ideal for baking, roasting, and broiling, techniques that yield depth of flavor with maximum ease and minimum effort.

The low sides and large, flat cooking surface of a sheet pan (a restaurant term for a rimmed baking sheet) allow the heat of the oven to reach the entire surface of foods as they cook. High, even heat quickly seals the exterior of the ingredients, drawing out their natural sugars so that they crisply brown on the outside while staying meltingly tender and tasty on the inside. This means that the flavor of meats as well as vegetables is intensified while their texture is enhanced—good news for vegetarians and for parents wanting their family to eat more vegetables.

Sheet-pan cooking is one-pan cooking: an entire meal can be prepared quickly and easily and then served straight from the oven. Because the ingredients cook fast and cleanup is simple, sheet-pan cooking is a great way to prepare family dinners, weeknight meals, and comfort foods. And it's also a smart choice if you're hosting a dinner party: the ingredients can be prepped in advance and then slipped into the oven while you spend time with your guests over appetizers and drinks.

The recipes in this book showcase the versatility of sheet-pan cooking, ranging from light and seasonal—Vegetable Pizza Tarts, Brussels Sprouts & Potato Hash with Baked Eggs, and Roasted Caesar Salad with Salmon—to heartier and more complex, such as Moroccan-Spiced Lamb Chops with Vegetable Kebabs & Cucumber Raita. Notable for their inspired combinations of fresh, nourishing ingredients, the recipes can also be customized—use them as guidelines and mix and match your favorites.

SHEET-PAN BASICS

Made of aluminum or stainless steel, sheet pans were originally designed for baked goods, such as cookies, rolls, and biscuits, but are equally well suited for savory dishes and are a mainstay for home cooks and chefs alike. Commonly known as rimmed or sided baking sheets, they may also be called jelly-roll pans, as they are traditionally used to make thin sheets of sponge cake. While restaurant-style sheet pans tend to be large (18 by 26 inches/45 by 66 cm), the ones used by home cooks are either small (12 $\frac{1}{2}$ by 8 $\frac{1}{4}$ inches/31.5 by 21 cm, known as quarter sheet pans) or standard (18 by 12 inches/45 by 30 cm, known as half sheet pans). Regardless of size, sheet pans are rectangular in shape and have rims that are 1 to 1$\frac{1}{2}$ inches (2.5 to 4 cm) high. All of the recipes in this book were made using one or two heavy-duty half sheet pans with a 1-inch (2.5-cm) rim.

TIPS FOR COOKING WITH SHEET PANS

- To use a sheet pan for baking, roasting, or broiling, first spray the pan with nonstick cooking spray. For even easier cleanup, spray the pan with nonstick cooking spray and line it with aluminum foil (for cooking meat) or parchment paper (for fish and vegetables). If using foil, then spray the foil lightly with nonstick cooking spray as well.

- In general, cut foods to about the same size and thickness so they will all cook evenly on the sheet pan in the same period of time. You can add different ingredients in batches to allow for varied cooking times. Spread the ingredients in the pan in a single layer to ensure that they cook evenly.

- Have a set of heavy metal tongs on hand; they're indispensable for turning over ingredients in the pan and for transferring foods from the pan to a serving platter or cutting board.

- Use a good-quality instant-read meat thermometer—it's the best way to test if meat is the perfect temperature.

- With some exceptions, many meats and vegetables need to be brushed, sprayed, or tossed with cooking oil or a marinade containing oil before baking, roasting, or broiling.

- Sheet pans are oven safe to 450°F (230°C).

- A pan with a 1-inch (2.5-cm) lip is essential: the lip seals in juices for flavor, keeps meat juicy, and helps reduce the chance of hot liquid spilling as the pan is removed from the oven.

- Make sure to preheat the oven to allow the heat to quickly seal the surface of the food. Most ovens take 15 to 30 minutes to preheat.

TIPS FOR CARING FOR SHEET PANS

- Sheet pans are dishwasher safe, but they may darken after repeated washings. If you want to preserve their original appearance, wash the pans by hand.

- Don't use abrasive cleaning products or scouring pads, as they will scratch the surface of the pans.

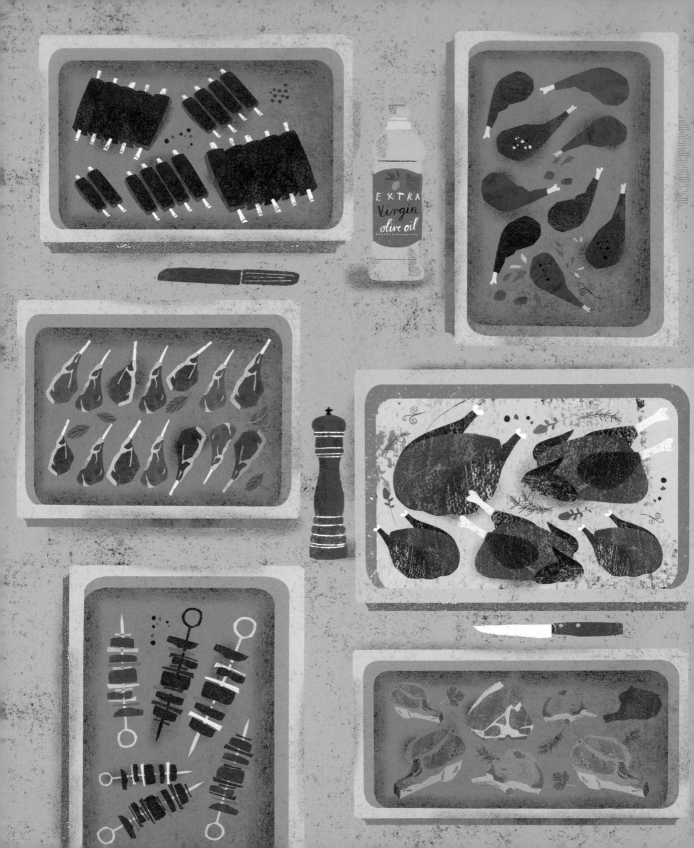

meat

21 Roasted Chicken with Giant Croutons, Sweet Potatoes & Arugula

22 Dijon-Rosemary Chicken Thighs with Maple-Glazed Pumpkin

24 Chicken Shawarma with Onions, Peppers & Tahini Sauce

25 Chicken Tikka Masala with Roasted Cauliflower & Red Onion

27 Chicken Drumsticks with Green Olives & Cipollini Onions

28 Chicken Schnitzel with Asparagus

29 Turkey Roulade with Sausage-Cornbread Stuffing & Kale

30 Spicy Asian Chicken Drumettes with Broccoli & Spiced Walnuts

33 Mexican Stuffed Peppers with Chipotle Sweet Potatoes

34 Vietnamese Turkey Meatball & Hoisin Eggplant Banh Mi

35 Meat Loaf with Roasted Mushrooms & Smashed Butternut Squash

37 Roasted Red Pepper, Spinach & Asiago Stuffed Flank Steak with Brown-Sugared Carrots

38 Oven Ribs with Mop Sauce & Pecorino-Jalapeño-Dusted Corn

40 Bangers & Smashed Potatoes with Whole-Grain Dijonnaise

41 Zucchini Bolognese al Forno

43 Herb-Crusted Beef Tenderloin with Ratatouille

44 Skirt Steak with Smoky Compound Butter & Blistered Shishito Peppers

45 Standing Rib Roast with Rosemary Root Vegetables & Horseradish Sauce

46 Pork Chops with Apricots, Red Cabbage & Blue Cheese

48 Asian Five-Spice Pork Tenderloin with Honey-Roasted Edamame

49 Pork Shoulder with Brussels Sprouts & Roasted Tomato Charmoula

51 Porchetta with Wilted Arugula & Warm Dates

52 Persian Stuffed Acorn Squash with Ground Lamb & Pomegranate

54 Spiced Lamb Patties with Orange-Thyme Tapenade & Baby Artichokes

55 Pork & Green Chile Empanadas with Broccoli Rabe

57 Moroccan-Spiced Lamb Chops with Vegetable Kebabs & Cucumber Raita

58 Bruschetta with Chili-Spiced Leg of Lamb & Caramelized Red Onions

This giant salad on a sheet pan is a beautiful and satisfying dinner. Croutons are especially delicious when toasted and then tossed in the meat juices and the vinaigrette from the arugula. Sweet potatoes and red onions, which roast alongside the chicken, round out the meal.

ROASTED CHICKEN WITH GIANT CROUTONS, SWEET POTATOES & ARUGULA

1 Preheat the oven to 400°F (200°C). Line a sheet pan with aluminum foil.

2 Brush the chicken with 2 tablespoons of the oil and place, breast side up, in the center of the prepared pan. Sprinkle the chicken with the oregano and thyme, and season generously with salt and pepper. Roast for 20 minutes.

3 In a medium bowl, toss together the sweet potatoes, onion, and 2 tablespoons of the oil. Place in a single layer around the chicken. Season the vegetables with salt and pepper, return the pan to the oven, and roast until the vegetables begin to soften, about 45 minutes, then stir the vegetables.

4 In a medium bowl, toss together the bread and the remaining 1 tablespoon oil, and season with salt and pepper. Scatter the bread all over the pan. Continue roasting until the bread is toasted, the chicken is opaque throughout, and the vegetables are fork-tender, about 10 minutes longer.

5 In another medium bowl, toss together the arugula and vinegar. Remove the baking sheet from the oven and carefully transfer the chicken to a cutting board and allow to rest. Immediately, while the vegetables are still hot, add the arugula to the sheet pan. Sprinkle the currants on top and gently toss the arugula with the vegetables and bread, allowing the arugula to wilt slightly.

6 Transfer the salad to a serving platter. Carefully cut the chicken into 10 pieces and lay the pieces on top of the salad. Serve right away.

1 chicken (about 4½ lb/ 2.25 kg)

5 tablespoons (80 ml) olive oil

1 teaspoon dried oregano

1 teaspoon dried thyme

Kosher salt and freshly ground pepper

3 small sweet potatoes (about 1½ lb/750 g), peeled and cut into 1-inch (2.5-cm) pieces

1 large red onion, cut into 6 wedges

½ loaf crusty Italian bread, cut into 1½-inch (4-cm) cubes (about 3 cups/185 g)

3 cups (3 oz/90 g) packed baby arugula

2 tablespoons red wine vinegar

¼ cup (1½ oz/45 g) dried currants

SERVES 4–6

This recipe features an enticing combination of sweet and savory ingredients. The chicken is roasted on the bone, which keeps the meat juicy and flavorful. You can rinse the pumpkin seeds and roast them with olive oil and salt for a snack or a crunchy addition to salads. When pumpkin isn't in season, swap in sweet potatoes or butternut squash.

DIJON-ROSEMARY CHICKEN THIGHS WITH MAPLE-GLAZED PUMPKIN

3 tablespoons Dijon mustard

5 tablespoons (80 ml) olive oil

1½ tablespoons balsamic vinegar

2 large cloves garlic, chopped

2 tablespoons chopped fresh rosemary

6 skin-on, bone-in chicken thighs (about 2½ lb/ 1.25 kg total)

5 shallots, halved lengthwise

1 small sugar pie pumpkin (about 2 lb/1 kg)

2 tablespoons pure maple syrup

Kosher salt and freshly ground pepper

SERVES 4–6

1 Preheat the oven to 400°F (200°C). Line a sheet pan with aluminum foil.

2 In a large bowl, whisk together the mustard, 3 tablespoons of the oil, the vinegar, garlic, and rosemary. Add the chicken and shallots and toss to coat. Let stand at room temperature while you prepare the pumpkin.

3 Cut off the top and bottom of the pumpkin, then cut it in half lengthwise and remove the seeds. Cut each half into 1-inch (2.5-cm) wedges. In another large bowl, stir together the maple syrup and the remaining 2 tablespoons oil. Add the pumpkin

and toss to combine. Place the pumpkin wedges in a single layer on one end of the prepared pan. Remove the chicken and shallots from the marinade and place on the other end of the pan. Season the chicken and pumpkin generously with salt and pepper.

4 Roast until the chicken is opaque throughout and the pumpkin is golden brown and soft, about 45 minutes. Serve right away.

Warmly spiced chicken and vegetables make a wonderful Middle Eastern dinner, especially when served with homemade tahini sauce. If you are short on time, replace the tahini sauce with store-bought hummus.

CHICKEN SHAWARMA WITH ONIONS, PEPPERS & TAHINI SAUCE

6 tablespoons (90 ml) olive oil

Juice of 1 lemon

2 cloves garlic, chopped

1½ teaspoons ground cumin

¾ teaspoon ground turmeric

¾ teaspoon paprika

Kosher salt and freshly ground pepper

1½ lb (750 g) skinless, boneless chicken breasts, cut into ½-inch (12-mm) slices

1 red and 1 yellow bell pepper, seeded and sliced into ½-inch-thick (12-mm) slices

1 red onion, halved and sliced into ½-inch-thick (12-mm) slices

FOR THE TAHINI SAUCE

1 clove garlic

½ cup (5 oz/155 g) tahini

Juice of 1 lemon

½ teaspoon ground cumin

Kosher salt

½ cup (120 ml) warm water

6 pieces lavash or pita bread, warmed (optional)

SERVES 4–6

1 In a large bowl, whisk together 4 tablespoons (60 ml) of the oil, the lemon juice, garlic, cumin, turmeric, paprika, 1 teaspoon salt, and ½ teaspoon pepper. Add the chicken and toss to coat. Cover and refrigerate for at least 2 hours or up to overnight.

2 Preheat the oven to 400°F (200°C). Line a sheet pan with aluminum foil.

3 Remove the chicken from the marinade and place in a single layer on one end of the prepared pan. In another bowl, toss together the bell peppers, onion, and the remaining 2 tablespoons oil. Place the vegetables in a single layer on the other end of the pan. Season the chicken and vegetables with salt and pepper. Roast, stirring once, until the chicken is opaque throughout and the vegetables are fork-tender, 25–30 minutes.

4 Meanwhile, prepare the tahini sauce: In a food processor or blender, combine the garlic, tahini, lemon juice, cumin, and ¼ teaspoon salt and purée until well blended. Add the warm water and purée until smooth. Adjust the seasoning with salt.

5 Fill the lavash, if using, with the chicken and vegetables, drizzle with the tahini sauce, and serve.

Indian food is traditionally paired with a cooling yogurt sauce, which here gets a kick from smoked paprika and cumin. You can replace the boneless thighs with drumsticks or bone-in breasts, although the cooking time will increase.

CHICKEN TIKKA MASALA WITH ROASTED CAULIFLOWER & RED ONION

1 In a large nonaluminum bowl, whisk together the yogurt, lemon juice, ginger, garlic, tomato paste, garam masala, cumin, paprika, cayenne, and 1 teaspoon salt. Add the chicken and toss to coat. Cover and refrigerate for at least 2 hours or up to 6 hours.

2 Preheat the oven to 425°F (220°C). Line a sheet pan with aluminum foil.

3 Remove the chicken from the marinade and transfer to the prepared pan, spreading the pieces out on the pan in a single layer. Roast for 10 minutes.

4 In another large bowl, toss together the cauliflower, onion, and oil. Place in a single layer around the chicken. Season the vegetables generously with salt and black pepper. Roast until the cauliflower begins to brown, about 20 minutes, then stir the vegetables. Continue roasting until the chicken is opaque throughout and the cauliflower is fork-tender, 10–15 minutes longer.

5 Meanwhile, prepare the paprika-yogurt sauce: In a small bowl, stir together the yogurt, garlic, oil, smoked paprika, and cumin, and season with salt. Dollop the sauce on top of the chicken and serve right away with the vegetables alongside.

1 cup (8 oz/250 g) plain whole-milk Greek yogurt

Juice of ½ lemon

1½-inch (4-cm) piece fresh ginger, peeled and grated

2 cloves garlic, chopped

1 tablespoon tomato paste

1½ teaspoons garam masala

1 teaspoon ground cumin

½ teaspoon *each* paprika and cayenne pepper

Kosher salt and freshly ground black pepper

6 skinless, boneless chicken thighs (about 2½ lb/1.25 kg total)

1 head cauliflower, cut into small florets

1 large red onion, cut into ½-inch (12-mm) pieces

¼ cup (60 ml) olive oil

FOR THE PAPRIKA-YOGURT SAUCE

1¼ cups (10 oz/315 g) plain whole-milk Greek yogurt

1 clove garlic, minced

2 teaspoons olive oil

1½ teaspoons smoked paprika

½ teaspoon ground cumin

SERVES 4–6

Cipollini onions are incredibly flavorful when roasted, and because they are so small, you'll want to leave them whole. To peel the onions, immerse in boiling water for 2 minutes, then drain and let cool slightly. The skins will slip right off. The brown sugar sweetens the dish and helps the chicken to become caramelized.

CHICKEN DRUMSTICKS WITH GREEN OLIVES & CIPOLLINI ONIONS

1 Preheat the oven to 375°F (190°C). Line a sheet pan with a piece of aluminum foil that is about 4 inches (10 cm) longer than the pan. Fold the sides up to create a border that will contain the marinade.

2 In a large bowl, combine the chicken, onions, olives, garlic, 3 tablespoons of the oil, the wine, and oregano. Season with salt and pepper and toss to combine. Place the chicken mixture on the prepared pan, spreading the ingredients out in a single layer. Drizzle the chicken with the remaining 1 tablespoon oil. Sprinkle the brown sugar over all and season again with salt. Roast until the chicken is opaque throughout and the onions are golden, about 40 minutes. Serve right away.

10 chicken drumsticks (about 2½ lb/1.25 kg total)

1 lb (500 g) cipollini onions, peeled

1 jar (10 oz/315 g) Spanish Queen olives, drained

4 cloves garlic, thinly sliced

4 tablespoons (60 ml) olive oil

¼ cup (60 ml) dry white wine

3 tablespoons chopped fresh oregano

Kosher salt and freshly ground pepper

3 tablespoons firmly packed dark brown sugar

SERVES 4–6

Schnitzel is a classic German dish that can be made with turkey, pork, veal, or chicken, as in this recipe. It's important to pound the meat to an even thickness so it will cook at the same rate and remain juicy throughout. To prevent the meat from tearing as you pound, place it between 2 sheets of plastic wrap.

CHICKEN SCHNITZEL WITH ASPARAGUS

6 skinless, boneless chicken breast halves (about 1/4 lb/125 g each)

Kosher salt and freshly ground pepper

1/2 cup (2 1/2 oz/75 g) all-purpose flour

2 large eggs

1 tablespoon Dijon mustard

1 cup (1 1/2 oz/45 g) panko bread crumbs

1 lb (500 g) asparagus, trimmed

2 tablespoons olive oil

2 teaspoons balsamic vinegar

2 tablespoons chopped fresh flat-leaf parsley

1 lemon, cut into 6 wedges

SERVES 4–6

1 Preheat the oven to 400°F (200°C). Line a sheet pan with parchment paper.

2 Working with 1 chicken breast at a time, place the chicken between 2 sheets of plastic wrap and gently pound to 1/4 inch (6 mm) thick. Season both sides of the chicken with salt and pepper and set aside.

3 Place the flour on a plate. In a bowl, whisk together the eggs and mustard. Place the panko on another plate. Dredge each piece of chicken in the flour, lightly coating both sides. Dip the chicken into the egg mixture,

letting the excess drip back into the bowl, and then coat in the panko. Place on one end of the prepared pan and roast for 10 minutes.

4 Toss together the asparagus, oil, and vinegar. Place in a single layer on the other end of the pan. Season the asparagus generously with salt and pepper. Continue roasting until the asparagus is fork-tender and the chicken is opaque throughout, about 10 minutes longer. Garnish with the parsley and lemon wedges and serve right away.

The roulade is tied with kitchen string to hold it together for even cooking and easier slicing. Keeping the skin attached to the turkey helps the meat stay moist, but be alert to the cooking time, as turkey dries out easily because of its low fat content.

TURKEY ROULADE WITH SAUSAGE-CORNBREAD STUFFING & KALE

1 Preheat the oven to 375°F (190°C). Line a sheet pan with aluminum foil.

2 In a large bowl, combine the cornbread, sausage, fennel seeds, garlic, and 1½ tablespoons of the oil. Season with salt and pepper and stir gently to mix.

3 Place the turkey breast, skin side down, between 2 sheets of plastic wrap and pound to an even thickness. Season the turkey with salt and pepper. Spread the stuffing over the turkey in a layer about ½ inch (12 mm) thick, leaving a 1-inch (2.5-cm) border. Roll up the turkey, taking care to keep the stuffing inside. Place, seam side down,

on the prepared pan. Using kitchen string, tie the breast in 4 different places. Brush the roulade with 1 tablespoon of the oil and season all over with salt and pepper. Roast for 45 minutes.

4 Place the kale on the pan next to the roulade, drizzle the kale with the remaining 1½ tablespoons oil, and season with salt and pepper. Continue roasting until the kale is wilted and an instant-read thermometer inserted into the thickest part of the roulade registers 165°F (74°C), about 10 minutes longer.

5 Snip the strings, cut the roulade into 1-inch (2.5-cm) slices, and serve the kale on the side.

3-by-4-inch (7.5-by-10-cm) piece prepared cornbread (about 2 cups/120 g crumbled)

½ lb (250 g) sweet Italian sausage, casing removed

2 teaspoons fennel seeds

2 cloves garlic, minced

4 tablespoons (60 ml) olive oil

Kosher salt and freshly ground pepper

1 skin-on, boneless turkey breast (about 2¾ lb/ 1.35 kg), butterflied

1 large bunch kale, thick stems removed, leaves cut into thirds

SERVES 4

Drumettes are always a crowd-pleaser, and this version is packed with delicious Asian flavors. The longer you marinate the meat, the tastier it will be, and the honey in the marinade will help the chicken to caramelize. For a milder dish, omit the Sriracha altogether, or increase the amount if you want more heat.

SPICY ASIAN CHICKEN DRUMETTES WITH BROCCOLI & SPICED WALNUTS

1½-inch (4-cm) piece fresh ginger, peeled and grated

3 cloves garlic, chopped

5 tablespoons (80 ml) plus 1½ teaspoons low-sodium soy sauce

3 tablespoons vegetable oil

3 tablespoons honey

2–3 teaspoons Sriracha chile sauce

2½ lb (1.25 kg) chicken drumettes

1 lb (500 g) broccoli, trimmed and cut into small florets

2 tablespoons olive oil

1 teaspoon dark sesame oil

Kosher salt

FOR THE SPICED WALNUTS

1½ tablespoons sugar

Kosher salt

¼ teaspoon ground cinnamon

⅛ teaspoon cayenne pepper

¾ cup (3 oz/90 g) walnuts

SERVES 4

1 In a large bowl, whisk together the ginger, garlic, the 5 tablespoons (80 ml) soy sauce, the vegetable oil, honey, and Sriracha. Add the chicken drumettes and toss to coat. Cover and refrigerate for at least 2 hours or up to overnight, stirring a few times to coat the chicken with the marinade.

2 Preheat the oven to 425°F (220°C). Lightly spray a sheet pan with nonstick cooking spray, line with aluminum foil, and spray again.

3 In another large bowl, toss together the broccoli, olive oil, the 1½ teaspoons soy sauce, and the sesame oil. Season with salt and set aside.

4 To prepare the spiced walnuts, in a small bowl, stir together the sugar, ½ teaspoon salt, the cinnamon, and

cayenne. In a medium bowl, toss the walnuts with 2 teaspoons water and then with the spice mixture. Set aside.

5 Remove the chicken from the marinade (reserving the marinade) and place on one end of the prepared pan. Roast for 20 minutes, then flip the chicken and brush with the reserved marinade. Place the broccoli on the other end of the pan (leaving room for the walnuts) and roast for 10 minutes. Stir the broccoli and place the walnuts in a single layer on the pan. Continue roasting until the chicken is opaque throughout, the broccoli is fork-tender, and the walnuts are toasted and deep brown, 5–8 minutes longer. Toss the broccoli with the walnuts and serve right away with the chicken.

This modern take on an old favorite comes together quickly, and Mexican-inspired fare is always a popular choice. It isn't necessary to cook either the filling or the peppers in advance, as 40 minutes in the oven will get the job done, keeping hands-on time to a minimum.

MEXICAN STUFFED PEPPERS WITH CHIPOTLE SWEET POTATOES

1 Preheat the oven to 375°F (190°C). Line a sheet pan with parchment paper.

2 Cut the bell peppers in half lengthwise (through the stem) and remove the seeds and membranes. Brush the pepper halves inside and out with 2 tablespoons of the oil. Place, cut side up, on one end of the prepared pan.

3 In a large bowl, combine the ground beef, garlic, tomato sauce, 2 tablespoons of the cilantro, the chili powder, cumin, ½ teaspoon salt, and ¼ teaspoon pepper. Stir gently to mix. Fill the pepper cavities with the beef mixture.

4 In a bowl, toss together the sweet potatoes, chipotle chiles, and the remaining 1 tablespoon oil. Place in a single layer on the other end of the pan. Roast, stirring the sweet potatoes halfway through cooking, until they are caramelized and fork-tender and the meat is cooked through, about 40 minutes. During the last 5 minutes of cooking, sprinkle the cheese over the peppers.

5 To serve, garnish the peppers with the remaining 2 tablespoons cilantro and a dollop of sour cream, if using. Serve right away with the sweet potatoes alongside.

3 bell peppers, preferably 3 different colors

3 tablespoons olive oil

1½ lb (750 g) lean ground beef

1 clove garlic, chopped

1¼ cups (310 ml) tomato sauce

4 tablespoons (¼ oz/7 g) packed fresh cilantro leaves, chopped

1 tablespoon plus 1 teaspoon chili powder

2 teaspoons ground cumin

Kosher salt and freshly ground pepper

2 sweet potatoes, peeled and sliced into ½-inch (12-mm) slices

1–2 chipotle chiles in adobo sauce, seeded and finely chopped

¾ cup (3 oz/90 g) shredded Monterey jack cheese

1 cup (8 oz/250 g) sour cream (optional)

SERVES 4

Banh mi is a Vietnamese street sandwich, usually made with pork, that explodes with flavor. You can use other meats instead, including beef or chicken. Pounding the lemongrass helps release its aromatic oils, imparting an authentic flavor.

VIETNAMESE TURKEY MEATBALL & HOISIN EGGPLANT BANH MI

1 cup (5 oz/155 g) shredded carrots

1/2 cup (2 oz/60 g) thinly sliced red onion

2 tablespoons rice vinegar

2 teaspoons sugar

2 lemongrass stalks, white part only

1/3 cup (1/3 oz/10 g) each fresh cilantro leaves and fresh mint leaves

1 lb (500 g) ground turkey (preferably dark meat)

1 large clove garlic, minced

2 tablespoons Asian fish sauce

Kosher salt

FOR THE HOISIN EGGPLANT

3 Japanese eggplants, cut lengthwise into thin slices

2 tablespoons canola oil

Kosher salt

1/4 cup (60 ml) hoisin sauce

2 teaspoons rice vinegar

1/2 teaspoon Sriracha chile sauce (optional)

4 soft hoagie rolls, halved lengthwise

SERVES 4

1 Preheat the oven to 375°F (190°C). Lightly spray a sheet pan with nonstick cooking spray, line with aluminum foil, and spray again.

2 In a nonaluminum bowl, stir together the carrots, onion, vinegar, and 1 teaspoon of the sugar. Let stand at room temperature.

3 Place the lemongrass on a cutting board and, using the flat side of a large knife, pound the stalks 4 or 5 times. Finely chop the lemongrass and place in a large bowl. Chop half of the cilantro and mint leaves and add to the bowl along with the ground turkey, garlic, fish sauce, and 1/4 teaspoon salt. Stir gently to mix. Form the mixture into 12 golf ball–size meatballs and place on one end of the prepared pan. Sprinkle the tops of the meatballs with the remaining 1 teaspoon sugar.

4 To prepare the eggplant, in another large bowl, toss together the eggplant and oil, and season with salt. Place the eggplant in a single layer on the other end of the pan. In a small bowl, stir together the hoisin sauce, vinegar, and Sriracha (if using). Brush the eggplant with half of the hoisin sauce mixture.

5 Roast for 10 minutes, then brush the eggplant with the remaining hoisin sauce mixture. Continue roasting until the meatballs are cooked through and the eggplant is fork-tender, about 10 minutes longer.

6 Just before serving, stir the remaining cilantro and mint leaves into the carrot mixture. Fill the rolls with the meatballs, eggplant, and pickled vegetables and serve right away.

We're guessing you've never made mashed vegetables on a sheet pan before, but this method is simple and makes cleanup a breeze. Here, meat loaf roasts alongside butternut squash and mushrooms, making for a complete single-pan supper.

MEAT LOAF WITH ROASTED MUSHROOMS & SMASHED BUTTERNUT SQUASH

1 Preheat the oven to 375°F (190°C). Lightly spray a sheet pan with nonstick cooking spray, line with aluminum foil, and spray again.

2 To prepare the meat loaf, in a large bowl, combine the bread crumbs, milk, and egg and let stand for 5 minutes. Add the garlic, shallot, the 2 tablespoons ketchup, Worcestershire sauce, ground beef, veal, and pork. Season generously with salt and pepper and stir gently just until combined; do not overmix. Using your hands, transfer the meat mixture to the prepared pan and form it into a loaf; it will be about the size of a brick. Bake for 45 minutes.

3 To prepare the mushrooms, in a medium bowl, toss together the mushrooms and butter (this is easiest using your hands), and season with salt and pepper. To prepare the butternut squash, in a large bowl, toss together

the squash and oil, and season with salt and pepper. Set aside.

4 Spread the ¼ cup (2 oz/60 g) ketchup over the top of the meat loaf. Place the mushrooms and squash side by side on the pan. Continue roasting, stirring the vegetables halfway through cooking, until the mushrooms are deep brown, the squash is golden and fork-tender, and an instant-read thermometer inserted into the center of the meat loaf registers 145°F (63°C), 25–30 minutes longer.

5 Using a potato masher or a large fork, smash the squash directly on the pan, then stir in the butter and adjust the seasoning with salt and pepper. Cut the meat loaf into slices and serve with the mushrooms and squash.

FOR THE MEAT LOAF

¾ cup (1½ oz/45 g) fresh bread crumbs

¼ cup (60 ml) milk

1 large egg, lightly beaten

2 cloves garlic, chopped

1 shallot, finely chopped

¼ cup (2 oz/60 g) plus 2 tablespoons ketchup

1½ tablespoons Worcestershire sauce

1 lb (500 g) ground beef

½ lb (250 g) each ground veal and ground pork

Kosher salt and freshly ground pepper

FOR THE ROASTED MUSHROOMS

1 lb (500 g) cremini mushrooms, brushed clean and halved

3 tablespoons unsalted butter, at room temperature

FOR THE BUTTERNUT SQUASH

14 oz (440 g) butternut squash, peeled and cut into 1-inch (2.5-cm) pieces

3 tablespoons olive oil

1 tablespoon unsalted butter, at room temperature

SERVES 4–6

Be sure to roll the stuffed flank steak with the grain. That way, you will be cutting the finished dish against the grain, which will yield more tender slices. Baby carrots look prettiest when you leave a little bit of the stem attached.

ROASTED RED PEPPER, SPINACH & ASIAGO STUFFED FLANK STEAK WITH BROWN-SUGARED CARROTS

1 Preheat the oven to 400°F (200°C). Line a sheet pan with parchment paper.

2 Lay the flank steak on a work surface so the grain is running left to right and season with salt and pepper. In a bowl, toss together the spinach and 2 teaspoons of the oil and arrange on the steak, leaving a 1-inch (2.5-cm) border. Sprinkle the cheese over the spinach and place the peppers in a single layer on top. Starting with the side closest to you, roll up the steak tightly, taking care to keep the stuffing inside. Place, seam side down, on one end of the prepared pan. Using kitchen string, tie the roll at 3-inch (8-cm) intervals. Brush the steak with the remaining 2 teaspoons oil and season all over with salt and pepper.

3 To ensure even cooking, cut any larger carrots in half lengthwise. In a small bowl, stir together the butter, brown sugar, and ½ teaspoon salt. Using your hands, spread the butter mixture all over the carrots and place on the other end of the pan.

4 Roast for 15 minutes and then toss the carrots. Continue roasting until the carrots are fork-tender and an instant-read thermometer inserted into the thickest part of the flank steak roll registers 125°F (52°C), 15–20 minutes longer. Transfer the steak to a cutting board, tent loosely with foil, and let rest for 10 minutes. Snip the strings and cut into 1-inch (2.5-cm) slices. Serve the carrots alongside.

1½ lb (750 g) flank steak, butterflied

Kosher salt and freshly ground pepper

3 cups (3 oz/90 g) packed spinach leaves

4 teaspoons olive oil

½ cup (2 oz/60 g) shredded Asiago cheese

2 small red bell peppers, roasted, seeded, and cut into 2-inch (5-cm) pieces

2 bunches baby carrots, peeled and stems trimmed

2 tablespoons unsalted butter, at room temperature

1½ tablespoons firmly packed dark brown sugar

SERVES 4

Ribs don't have to be complicated—they just need a flavorful rub and plenty of hands-off time in the oven. Mop sauce, a Southern barbecue staple that combines yellow mustard with a few other ingredients, is served as a dip alongside.

OVEN RIBS WITH MOP SAUCE & PECORINO-JALAPEÑO-DUSTED CORN

FOR THE RIBS

1 tablespoon firmly packed dark brown sugar

Kosher salt and freshly ground pepper

1½ teaspoons *each* ground cumin, paprika, onion powder, garlic powder, and chili powder

2 racks beef back ribs (7 ribs each)

FOR THE PECORINO-JALAPEÑO-DUSTED CORN

4 ears of corn

1½ tablespoons unsalted butter, at room temperature

¼ cup (1 oz/30 g) finely grated pecorino cheese

2 teaspoons seeded and finely chopped jalapeño chile

Freshly ground pepper

FOR THE MOP SAUCE

1 cup (8 oz/250 g) yellow mustard

¼ cup (3 oz/90 g) honey

¼ cup (2 oz/60 g) firmly packed dark brown sugar

¼ cup (60 ml) cider vinegar

Hot sauce, to taste

SERVES 4

1 Line a sheet pan with aluminum foil. Place 1 rack in the upper third and 1 rack in the lower third of the oven and preheat oven to 300°F (150°C).

2 To prepare the ribs, in a small bowl, stir together the brown sugar, 1 tablespoon salt, ½ teaspoon pepper, the cumin, paprika, onion powder, garlic powder, and chili powder. Remove the thin membrane from the back of each rib rack and trim off the excess fat. Massage the rub all over the ribs and place on the prepared pan. Roast on the upper rack until the meat is easily shredded from the bone, 2–2¼ hours.

3 To prepare the corn, remove the husks and silks from each cob. Rub the ears of corn with the butter, loosely wrap individually in aluminum foil, and place on another sheet pan. When the ribs have about 25 minutes left, transfer the corn to the oven and roast until fork-tender.

4 Meanwhile, in a small bowl, stir together the cheese and jalapeño and season with pepper. Spread the cheese mixture on a plate. When the corn is done, immediately remove the ears from the foil and roll in the cheese mixture.

5 To prepare the mop sauce, in a bowl, stir together the mustard, honey, brown sugar, vinegar, and hot sauce. Set aside at room temperature.

6 Transfer the ribs to a cutting board and cut between the bones. Serve with the mop sauce and corn on the side.

This just might be the easiest, most low-fuss dish in the book, but it's still big on flavor. Serve this classic English pub fare for a weeknight meal paired with a simple green salad. Leftover Dijonnaise is terrific spread on sandwiches the next day.

BANGERS & SMASHED POTATOES WITH WHOLE-GRAIN DIJONNAISE

1 1/2 lb (750 g) small Yukon gold potatoes

2 red onions, quartered

3 tablespoons olive oil

Kosher salt and freshly ground pepper

6 bangers or other beef or pork sausages

FOR THE DIJONNAISE

1/2 cup (4 oz/125 g) whole-grain Dijon mustard

3 tablespoons mayonnaise

1 tablespoon fresh lemon juice

SERVES 4–6

1 Preheat the oven to 450°F (230°C). Line a sheet pan with aluminum foil.

2 In a large bowl, toss together the potatoes, onions, and oil, and season generously with salt and pepper. Place the potatoes and onions in a single layer all over the prepared pan and roast for 10 minutes.

3 Nestle the sausages into the vegetables and roast for 15 minutes, then flip the sausages and stir the potatoes and onions. Continue roasting until the sausages are cooked through, the potatoes are fork-tender, and the onions are browned on the edges, about 10 minutes longer. Using a potato masher or a large fork, smash each potato so that the skin breaks and the soft center is exposed.

4 To prepare the Dijonnaise, in a small bowl, stir together the mustard, mayonnaise, and lemon juice, and season with salt and pepper. Serve the sausage, potatoes, and onions with the Dijonnaise alongside.

Simple to make, this dinner is Italian comfort food at its best. Lean ground beef, which produces less fat during cooking, is the best choice for this dish. For a delicious twist, use spicy bulk sausage instead. Add any extra stuffing to the pan to cook on its own; it's terrific scooped up with bread. Pour a Barolo alongside.

ZUCCHINI BOLOGNESE AL FORNO

1 Preheat the oven to 375°F (190°C). Line a sheet pan with aluminum foil.

2 Cut the zucchini in half lengthwise. Using a small spoon, gently scoop out the seeds from each half to create a pocket. Season the zucchini with salt and place, cut side up, on the prepared pan.

3 In a large bowl, combine the ground beef, pork, basil, fennel seeds, red pepper flakes, ½ cup (3½ oz/105 g) of the tomatoes, ¼ cup (1 oz/30 g) of the cheese, 1 teaspoon salt, and ½ teaspoon black pepper. Stir gently to mix.

4 Divide the meat mixture among the zucchini halves, mounding the mixture on top of each, and roast for 25 minutes. Top each zucchini half with 1 tablespoon of the remaining tomatoes and 1 tablespoon of the remaining cheese. Continue roasting until the cheese is melted and the meat is cooked through, about 5 minutes longer. Serve right away.

4 zucchini (about 1½ lb/ 750 g total)

Kosher salt and freshly ground black pepper

¾ lb (375 g) lean ground beef

½ lb (250 g) ground pork

2 tablespoons chopped fresh basil

1½ teaspoons fennel seeds

½ teaspoon red pepper flakes

1 cup (7 oz/220 g) canned crushed tomatoes

¾ cup (3 oz/90 g) grated Parmesan cheese

SERVES 4

You will taste a world of difference in your cooking by using fresh homemade bread crumbs. It really is as easy as placing day-old bread in a food processor and pulsing until fine crumbs form. The layer of mustard on the tenderloin helps to keep the meat juicy—a must for this lean and tender cut.

HERB-CRUSTED BEEF TENDERLOIN WITH RATATOUILLE

1 Let the beef tenderloin stand at room temperature for 45 minutes.

2 Preheat the oven to 450°F (230°C). Line a sheet pan with aluminum foil.

3 Place the tenderloin on one end of the prepared pan and season with salt and pepper. In a small bowl, stir together the bread crumbs and parsley, and season with salt and pepper. Using a rubber spatula, spread the mustard all over the top and sides of the tenderloin. Using your hands, pat the bread crumb mixture evenly over the mustard.

4 To prepare the ratatouille, in a large bowl, stir together the squash, zucchini, eggplant, cherry tomatoes, oil, and vinegar. Place the vegetables in a single layer on the other end of the pan and season generously with salt and pepper.

5 Roast, stirring the vegetables halfway through cooking, until an instant-read thermometer inserted into the center of the meat registers 130°F (54°C) for medium-rare, and the vegetables are fork-tender, 35–40 minutes. Remove the pan from the oven, tent with foil, and let the tenderloin rest for 10 minutes.

6 Transfer the tenderloin to a cutting board and cut into 1-inch (2.5-cm) slices. Stir the basil into the ratatouille, drizzle with oil, and adjust the seasoning with salt and pepper. Dollop pieces of the cheese over the ratatouille and serve alongside the beef.

1 beef tenderloin (about 2 lb/1 kg), trimmed

Kosher salt and freshly ground pepper

1¼ cups (2½ oz/75 g) fresh bread crumbs

⅓ cup (⅓ oz/10 g) fresh flat-leaf parsley leaves, finely chopped

2½ tablespoons Dijon mustard

FOR THE RATATOUILLE

2 small yellow squash, cut into ¾-inch (2-cm) pieces

2 small zucchini, cut into ¾-inch (2-cm) pieces

½ eggplant, cut into ¾-inch (2-cm) pieces

1 cup (6 oz/185 g) cherry tomatoes

⅓ cup (80 ml) olive oil, plus more for drizzling

2 tablespoons red wine vinegar

Kosher salt and freshly ground pepper

2 tablespoons chopped fresh basil

3 oz (90 g) goat cheese, at room temperature

SERVES 4–6

Compound butters are a great way to add a flavor boost to almost any dish, and the combinations are endless: try orange zest and parsley, or jalapeño and lime. Japanese shishito peppers are sweet with almost no spicy heat.

SKIRT STEAK WITH SMOKY COMPOUND BUTTER & BLISTERED SHISHITO PEPPERS

1¹/₂ lb (750 g) skirt steak

3 tablespoons olive oil

Kosher salt and freshly ground pepper

4 tablespoons (2 oz/60 g) unsalted butter, at room temperature

¹/₈ teaspoon smoked paprika

³/₄ lb (375 g) shishito peppers

SERVES 4

1 Position a rack 4–6 inches (10–15 cm) from the heat source and preheat the broiler. Line a sheet pan with aluminum foil.

2 Cut the skirt steak crosswise into 3 or 4 pieces (this will make it easier to slice for serving). Brush the steak on both sides with 1 tablespoon of the oil and season with salt and pepper. Let stand at room temperature.

3 In a small bowl, stir together the butter and paprika and season with salt. Using a rubber spatula, spread the butter onto a piece of parchment paper and roll it up to form a log. If the butter is too soft, refrigerate it. You want to be able to slice it, but it shouldn't be too cold.

4 In a medium bowl, toss together the shishito peppers and the remaining 2 tablespoons oil, and season generously with salt and pepper. Place the steak on one end of the prepared pan and the peppers on the other end and broil for 3 minutes. Flip the steak and stir the peppers and continue broiling for 3 minutes longer. Remove from the oven and immediately season the peppers again with salt.

5 Transfer the steak to a cutting board and let rest for a few minutes, then slice against the grain. Cut the compound butter into slices and place on top of the steak. Serve right away with the peppers on the side.

This recipe requires two sheet pans, but the effort is worth it. The vegetables need to roast at a much higher temperature than the beef so they will emerge deliciously caramelized. Roast them while the meat rests before slicing it.

STANDING RIB ROAST WITH ROSEMARY ROOT VEGETABLES & HORSERADISH SAUCE

1 Let the rib roast stand at room temperature for 1 hour.

2 Preheat the oven to 450°F (230°C). Line a sheet pan with aluminum foil.

3 Place the roast, ribs down, on the prepared pan and brush with 2 tablespoons of the oil. Sprinkle the roast all over with the garlic and season with salt and pepper.

4 Roast until the meat is browned, about 25 minutes. Reduce the oven temperature to 350°F (180°C) and continue roasting until an instant-read thermometer inserted into the center of the meat registers 125°F (52°C) for rare, 1¼–1½ hours longer. Transfer the roast to a cutting board, tent with foil, and let rest while you cook the vegetables.

5 Raise the oven temperature to 450°F (230°C). Line another sheet pan with parchment paper. In a large bowl, toss together the sweet potatoes, parsnips, rutabaga, and the remaining 4 tablespoons oil. Place the vegetables in a single layer on the prepared pan. Sprinkle with the rosemary, salt, and pepper. Roast, stirring the vegetables once halfway through cooking, until they are browned and fork-tender, 20–25 minutes.

6 Meanwhile, prepare the horseradish sauce: In a small bowl, stir together the horseradish, sour cream, mustard, and lemon juice, and season with salt and pepper. Set aside at room temperature.

7 Cut the roast into slices and serve with the vegetables and horseradish sauce on the side.

3-rib standing beef rib roast (about 7 lb/3.5 kg)

6 tablespoons (90 ml) olive oil

3 cloves garlic, finely chopped

Kosher salt and freshly ground pepper

2 sweet potatoes, peeled and cut into ½-inch (12-mm) pieces

2 parsnips, peeled and cut into ½-inch (12-mm) pieces

1 large rutabaga, peeled and cut into ½-inch (12-mm) pieces

2½ tablespoons chopped fresh rosemary

FOR THE HORSERADISH SAUCE

⅓ cup (5 g) grated peeled fresh horseradish

1 cup (8 oz/250 g) sour cream

1 tablespoon plus 1 teaspoon Dijon mustard

Juice of ½ lemon

Kosher salt and freshly ground pepper

SERVES 6

Sweet, savory, and salty components come together for a perfect combination in this impressive but simple dish. Cooking pork on the bone yields a richer flavor, and be sure to season the chops with plenty of salt and pepper; it enhances the taste of the meat. Serve this dish with a dry Sauvignon Blanc or a fruity Pinot Noir.

PORK CHOPS WITH APRICOTS, RED CABBAGE & BLUE CHEESE

6 cups (18 oz/560 g) shredded red cabbage (about ³/₄ head)

¹/₄ cup (60 ml) plus 2 tablespoons olive oil

3 tablespoons balsamic vinegar

Kosher salt and freshly ground pepper

4 apricots, halved and pitted

4 bone-in, center-cut pork chops (about 3 lb/ 1.5 kg total)

¹/₄ lb (125 g) blue cheese, crumbled

SERVES 4

1 Preheat the oven to 400°F (200°C). Line a sheet pan with aluminum foil.

2 In a large bowl, toss together the cabbage, the ¹/₄ cup (60 ml) oil, and the vinegar, and season generously with salt and pepper. Place the cabbage on one end of the prepared pan, spreading it out in an even layer. Add the apricots to the bowl and toss gently in the remaining oil and vinegar. Place, cut side up, on the bed of cabbage.

3 Brush both sides of the pork chops with the 2 tablespoons oil and season generously with salt and pepper. Place the chops on the other end of the pan.

4 Roast until an instant-read thermometer inserted into the center of the chops registers 145°F (63°C) and the cabbage is fork-tender, 35–40 minutes. During the last 5 minutes of cooking, sprinkle the blue cheese over the cabbage and apricots. Let rest for a few minutes and then serve.

This dish comes together so quickly that you may want to roast a second tenderloin and make sandwiches the next day, or wrap the meat in flour tortillas and serve with mango salsa. The honey-roasted edamame are memorable and well worth getting your fingers messy.

ASIAN FIVE-SPICE PORK TENDERLOIN WITH HONEY-ROASTED EDAMAME

1 pork tenderloin (about 1¼ lb/625 g)

4 teaspoons vegetable or canola oil

2 teaspoons Chinese five-spice powder

Kosher salt

1 lb (500 g) fresh or thawed frozen edamame in the shell

2½ tablespoons honey

2 tablespoons low-sodium soy sauce

1 clove garlic, minced

¼ teaspoon red pepper flakes (optional)

SERVES 4

1 Preheat the oven to 400°F (200°C). Line a sheet pan with aluminum foil.

2 Brush the pork tenderloin all over with 2 teaspoons of the oil and season with the five-spice powder and salt. Place on one end of the prepared pan and roast for 10 minutes.

3 In a bowl, toss together the edamame, honey, soy sauce, garlic, red pepper flakes (if using), and the remaining 2 teaspoons oil. Place the edamame on the other end of the pan. Continue roasting, stirring the edamame halfway through cooking, until they are caramelized and an instant-read thermometer inserted into the center of the meat registers 145°F (63°C), 15–20 minutes longer. Transfer to a cutting board, tent with aluminum foil, and let rest for 10 minutes before slicing.

This recipe yields a ton of shredded meat, but you'll be thrilled to have leftovers for making tacos later in the week. The pork is roasted simply, with just olive oil, garlic, salt, and pepper, but the charmoula, a North African sauce that's spooned over the meat, really makes this dish sing. Extra charmoula is terrific with scrambled eggs.

PORK SHOULDER WITH BRUSSELS SPROUTS & ROASTED TOMATO CHARMOULA

1 Preheat the oven to 425°F (220°C). Line a sheet pan with aluminum foil.

2 Place the pork shoulder in the center of the prepared pan and coat with 2 tablespoons of the oil and the garlic. Season generously with salt and pepper. Roast for 20 minutes, then reduce the oven temperature to 325°F (165°C). Continue roasting until the meat shreds easily and an instant-read thermometer inserted into the center registers 145°F (63°C), about 3 hours longer. Transfer the pork to a cutting board, tent with foil, and let rest for 30 minutes.

3 Raise the oven temperature to 500°F (260°C). Line another sheet pan with parchment paper. In a large bowl, toss together the brussels sprouts and 2 tablespoons of the oil, and season generously with salt and pepper.

Place in a single layer on one end of the prepared pan. Brush the tomatoes with 1 tablespoon of the oil and season with salt and pepper. Place, cut side down, on the other end of the pan. Roast until the tomatoes begin to char, about 10 minutes. Transfer the tomatoes to a cutting board. Stir the brussels sprouts and continue roasting until they are fork-tender, about 7 minutes longer. Tent the brussels sprouts with foil while you finish the charmoula.

4 When the tomatoes are cool enough to handle, cut into 1/2-inch (12-mm) pieces. Transfer to a bowl and stir in the remaining 1 tablespoon oil, the cilantro, parsley, cumin, and lemon zest and juice. Season with salt and pepper.

5 Shred the pork shoulder using 2 forks. Serve with the charmoula and brussels sprouts on the side.

1 boneless pork shoulder roast (about 4 lb/2 kg) (preferably with a layer of fat intact)

6 tablespoons (90 ml) olive oil

3 cloves garlic, finely chopped

Kosher salt and freshly ground pepper

1 lb (500 g) brussels sprouts, trimmed and halved lengthwise

4 Roma tomatoes, halved lengthwise

1/4 cup (1/4 oz/7 g) loosely packed fresh cilantro leaves, chopped

1/4 cup (1/4 oz/7 g) loosely packed fresh flat-leaf parsley leaves, chopped

1/2 teaspoon ground cumin

Zest and juice of 1/2 lemon

SERVES 6

What could be tastier than wrapping pork in more pork! Besides adding great flavor, the prosciutto gives the pork loin a crispy exterior and holds in moisture during roasting. Be sure to toss the arugula with the meat juices on the pan, which will add depth to this wilted salad.

PORCHETTA WITH WILTED ARUGULA & WARM DATES

1 Preheat the oven to 450°F (230°C). Line a sheet pan with aluminum foil.

2 Lay the pork loin, cut side up, on a work surface, and season with salt and pepper. In a bowl, stir together the bread crumbs, garlic, rosemary, sage, fennel seeds, and 2 tablespoons of the oil, and season with salt and pepper. Spread the bread crumb mixture in an even layer over the pork, leaving a 1-inch (2.5-cm) border.

3 Lay the prosciutto on another work surface, overlapping the slices to form a bed wide and long enough that will completely enclose the pork loin. Starting with a long side, roll up the pork loin and place it, seam side up, on top of the prosciutto. Keeping one hand on the pork so that it doesn't unroll, wrap the prosciutto around it, taking care that the prosciutto adheres to the meat. Carefully place the pork, seam side down, in the center of the prepared pan. Season with salt and pepper and roast for 25 minutes.

4 Reduce the oven temperature to 300°F (150°C) and continue roasting until an instant-read thermometer inserted into the center of the meat registers 145°F (63°C), about 45 minutes longer.

5 Just before removing the pork from the oven, in a bowl, toss together the arugula, dates, and the remaining 2 tablespoons oil, and season with salt and pepper. Remove the pan from the oven and immediately scatter the arugula mixture all around the pork; the arugula will wilt from the residual heat. Let the pork rest for 10 minutes.

6 Transfer the pork to a cutting board and cut into slices. Place the arugula and dates on a platter and top with the pork. Serve right away.

1 boneless pork loin (about 3 1/2 lb/1.75 kg), butterflied

Kosher salt and freshly ground pepper

1 1/2 cups (3 oz/90 g) fresh bread crumbs

2 cloves garlic, chopped

2 tablespoons chopped fresh rosemary

2 tablespoons chopped fresh sage

1 tablespoon fennel seeds

4 tablespoons (60 ml) olive oil

10 thin slices prosciutto

5 oz (155 g) baby arugula

1 cup (8 oz/230 g) dates, pitted and halved

SERVES 6

Acorn squash halves make an excellent vessel for a hearty dish, and you can swap in any ground meat for the lamb. Roasting the squash halves before filling them with the meat mixture ensures they will be completely tender. Pomegranate seeds add color and crunch. To round out the meal, serve a simple green salad with a citrus vinaigrette.

PERSIAN STUFFED ACORN SQUASH WITH GROUND LAMB & POMEGRANATE

2 acorn squash, halved lengthwise and seeded

3 tablespoons olive oil

Kosher salt and freshly ground pepper

1¹⁄₃ lb (21 oz/655 g) ground lamb

Zest of 1¹⁄₂ lemons

¹⁄₂ small yellow onion, grated

3 cloves garlic, minced

3 tablespoons chopped fresh flat-leaf parsley

3 tablespoons chopped fresh mint, plus whole leaves for garnish

1 tablespoon ground cumin

1 tablespoon ground coriander

¹⁄₄ teaspoon ground cinnamon

³⁄₄ cup (6 oz/185 g) plain whole-milk yogurt

1¹⁄₂ tablespoons fresh lemon juice

¹⁄₄ cup (1 oz/30 g) pomegranate seeds

SERVES 4

1 Preheat the oven to 400°F (200°C). Line a sheet pan with parchment paper.

2 Place the squash halves, cut side up, on the prepared pan. Brush the squash inside and out with 2 tablespoons of the oil, and season the cavities with salt and pepper. Roast until the squash is golden and fork-tender, about 30 minutes.

3 In a large bowl, combine the ground lamb, lemon zest, onion, garlic, parsley, 2 tablespoons of the mint, the cumin, coriander, cinnamon, and the remaining 1 tablespoon oil. Season with salt and pepper and stir gently to mix.

4 Fill the squash cavities with the lamb mixture and continue roasting until the meat is cooked through, 15–18 minutes longer. Let cool slightly.

5 In a small bowl, stir together the, lemon juice, and the remaining 1 tablespoon mint, and season with salt and pepper. Drizzle the yogurt sauce over the squash. Garnish with the pomegranate seeds and mint leaves and serve.

Baby artichokes are really quite easy to prepare and are especially delicious when roasted. Serve them alongside these lamb patties or as an appetizer on their own with a simple aioli. If you have any leftover tapenade, refrigerate it for up to 2 weeks and enjoy with roasted meats or on a baguette.

SPICED LAMB PATTIES WITH ORANGE-THYME TAPENADE & BABY ARTICHOKES

1¼ lb (625 g) ground lamb

2 cloves garlic, finely chopped

2½ teaspoons ground cumin

1½ teaspoons ground coriander

¾ teaspoon paprika

Kosher salt and freshly ground pepper

FOR THE ORANGE-THYME TAPENADE

1½ cups (7½ oz/235 g) pitted Kalamata olives, roughly chopped

1 tablespoon olive oil

2 tablespoons grated orange zest

1 tablespoon chopped fresh thyme

Freshly ground pepper

Juice of ½ lemon

1 lb (500 g) baby artichokes

2 tablespoons olive oil

SERVES 4

1 Preheat the oven to 400°F (200°C). Line a sheet pan with parchment paper.

2 In a large bowl, combine the ground lamb, garlic, cumin, coriander, paprika, 1 teaspoon salt, and ½ teaspoon pepper. Stir gently to mix. Form the mixture into 12 patties and season the tops with salt. Set aside.

3 To prepare the tapenade, in a bowl, toss together the olives, oil, orange zest, and thyme, and season with pepper. Set aside.

4 Fill a nonaluminum bowl with water and add the lemon juice. Working with 1 artichoke at a time, cut off the top and most of the stem. Peel away the tough outer leaves until you reach the light yellow heart. Using a vegetable peeler, trim the stem and base of the artichoke. Cut the artichoke into quarters and drop into the bowl of lemon water. When you have finished, drain the artichokes, toss with the oil, and season generously with salt and pepper. Place the artichokes in a single layer on one end of the prepared pan and roast for 12 minutes.

5 Stir the artichokes and place the lamb patties and tapenade on the other end of the pan. Continue roasting until the lamb is medium-rare, the artichokes are fork-tender, and the tapenade is warmed through, 12–15 minutes longer. Serve right away.

This recipe calls for using half a box of puff pastry. But do yourself a favor and double the recipe, then freeze half of the unbaked empanadas for a future meal (they freeze beautifully). Just before baking, brush the frozen empanadas with the egg mixture and increase the baking time by 5 to 6 minutes.

PORK & GREEN CHILE EMPANADAS WITH BROCCOLI RABE

1 Preheat the oven to 425°F (220°C). Line two sheet pans with parchment paper.

2 In a bowl, toss together the broccoli rabe and oil, and season with salt and pepper. Place the broccoli rabe in a single layer on one of the prepared pans and set aside.

3 In a large bowl, combine the ground pork, garlic, chiles, cumin, 3/4 teaspoon salt, and 1/4 teaspoon pepper and stir gently to mix.

4 On a lightly floured work surface, roll out the puff pastry into a 12-inch (30-cm) square. Cut into 4 equal squares. Place one-fourth of the pork mixture in the center of each square and

brush the outer edges with the egg mixture. Fold over diagonally, using your fingers to spread the meat out under the top layer of pastry. Using a fork, crimp the edges to seal and prick the top of the pastry in 3 places to create vents. Transfer to the other prepared pan, brush the tops with the egg mixture, and bake for 5 minutes.

5 Once the empanadas have baked for 5 minutes, add the broccoli rabe to the oven. If your sheet pans will fit in the oven side by side, put them on the same rack; if not, place the broccoli rabe on the rack below the empanadas. Bake until the broccoli rabe is fork-tender and the empanadas are golden brown, about 15 minutes. Serve right away.

1 bunch broccoli rabe, thick stems trimmed

2 tablespoons olive oil

Kosher salt and freshly ground pepper

1 lb (500 g) ground pork

2 cloves garlic, finely chopped

3 tablespoons canned green chiles, drained then measured

1 tablespoon ground cumin

All-purpose flour, for dusting

1 sheet frozen puff pastry (half of a 17.3-oz/490-g package), thawed

1 large egg beaten with 1 tablespoon water

SERVES 4

Popular in India, raita is a cooling combination of yogurt and vegetables. There are endless variations, making it wonderfully versatile—it can be served as a relish, dip, salad, or side with meat or fish. If you can't find naan, substitute lavash or pita bread.

MOROCCAN-SPICED LAMB CHOPS WITH VEGETABLE KEBABS & CUCUMBER RAITA

1 If using wooden skewers, soak 8–10 skewers in water for at least 30 minutes.

2 In a small bowl, stir together the cumin, cardamom, ginger, cayenne, and ½ teaspoon salt. Sprinkle the garlic on one side of the lamb chops and coat both sides with the spice mixture. Let the chops stand at room temperature for 30 minutes.

3 Preheat the oven to 375°F (190°C). Line a sheet pan with aluminum foil.

4 To prepare the cucumber raita, in a bowl, stir together the yogurt, cucumber, lemon juice, cumin, and mint. Season with salt and black pepper. Set aside.

5 In a large bowl, toss together the bell pepper, zucchini, squash, onion, 2 tablespoons of the oil, and the vinegar. Season generously with salt and black pepper. Thread the vegetables onto the

skewers, alternating as you go, and place on one end of the prepared pan. Roast until the vegetables begin to soften, about 10 minutes.

6 Flip the skewers and place the lamb chops on the other end of the pan. Continue roasting until the lamb is medium-rare and the vegetables are fork-tender, about 20 minutes. Brush the naan on one side with the remaining 2 tablespoons oil and season with salt. During the last 2 minutes of cooking, add the naan to the outside corners of the pan; it's okay if they overlap with the other food.

7 Serve the lamb chops with the kebabs and naan, and pass the cucumber raita at the table.

1 tablespoon ground cumin

1 teaspoon ground cardamom

½ teaspoon *each* ground ginger and cayenne pepper

Kosher salt and freshly ground black pepper

2 cloves garlic, minced

12 lamb rib chops (about 3 oz/90 g each)

FOR THE CUCUMBER RAITA

1½ cups (12 oz/375 g) plain whole milk Greek yogurt

1 small cucumber, peeled, seeded, and finely diced

Juice of 1 lemon

¾ teaspoon ground cumin

2 tablespoons chopped fresh mint

1 red bell pepper, seeded and cut into 1-inch (2.5-cm) pieces

1 zucchini and 1 yellow squash, each cut into 1-inch (2.5-cm) pieces

½ red onion, cut into 1-inch (2.5-cm) pieces

4 tablespoons (60 ml) olive oil

1½ tablespoons balsamic vinegar

4 pieces naan

SERVES 4

A roasted leg of lamb is one of the most impressive dishes, but the truth is, it couldn't be easier to make. Your one job is to ensure that it doesn't overcook, so invest in a good instant-read thermometer and test in the thickest part of the meat. This dish is great for entertaining because you can let guests assemble their own bruschetta.

BRUSCHETTA WITH CHILI-SPICED LEG OF LAMB & CARAMELIZED RED ONIONS

1 boneless leg of lamb
(5$\frac{1}{2}$–6 lb/2.75–3 kg)

7 tablespoons (105 ml)
olive oil

1$\frac{1}{2}$ tablespoons
chili powder

Kosher salt and freshly
ground pepper

4 red onions, halved and cut
into $\frac{1}{2}$-inch (12-mm) slices

2$\frac{1}{2}$ tablespoons balsamic
vinegar

2 teaspoons firmly packed
dark brown sugar

1 loaf crusty Italian bread,
such as ciabatta or batard,
cut into $\frac{1}{2}$-inch (12-mm)
slices

1 clove garlic, halved
lengthwise

$\frac{3}{4}$ cup (6 fl oz/180 ml)
mayonnaise

2 tablespoons Sriracha
chile sauce

SERVES 8–10

1 Let the leg of lamb stand at room temperature for 45 minutes.

2 Preheat the oven to 450°F (230°C). Line a sheet pan with aluminum foil.

3 Place the lamb on the prepared pan, cut side down (you want the spice mixture on the outside once you roll), and brush with 2 tablespoons of the oil. In a small bowl, stir together the chili powder, 1 teaspoon salt, and $\frac{1}{2}$ teaspoon pepper. Rub the spice mixture all over the lamb then turn it over so that it's cut side down. Beginning with the long side of the lamb, roll it up and place it seam side down. Using kitchen string, tie the lamb at 1-inch (2.5-cm) intervals. Roast for 30 minutes.

4 In a bowl, toss together the onions, 3 tablespoons of the oil, and the vinegar, and season with salt and pepper. Spread the onions around the lamb and roast for 20 minutes. Stir the onions, sprinkle with the brown sugar, and

continue roasting until an instant-read thermometer inserted into the center of the meat registers 125°F (52°C) for rare, and the onions are fork-tender and caramelized, 15–20 minutes longer. Transfer the lamb to a cutting board, tent with foil, and let rest for 15 minutes.

5 Position a rack 4–6 inches (10–15 cm) from the heat source and preheat the broiler. Brush one side of the bread slices with the remaining 2 tablespoons oil and season with salt and pepper. Place, oiled side up, on a clean sheet pan. Broil until the bread is toasted, about 3 minutes. Remove the pan from the oven and immediately rub the top of each slice with the cut side of the garlic.

6 In a small bowl, stir together the mayonnaise and Sriracha and season with salt. Snip the strings and cut the lamb into thin slices. Slather the mayonnaise on the bruschetta, top with the lamb and onions, and serve.

seafood

65 Ahi Tuna Niçoise Salad
with Olive Oil–Dill Aioli

66 Garlicky Shrimp
with Asparagus Fries
& Meyer Lemon Aioli

68 Roasted Mussels
with Tomatoes, Fennel
& Buttery Bread Crumbs

69 Roasted Scallops
with Spinach & Lemons

70 Whole Roasted Fish
with Fennel, Lemons
& Chimichurri Sauce

73 Oven Paella with Chorizo,
Clams & Shrimp

74 Salmon Provençal
with Fingerling Potatoes
& Cherry Tomatoes

76 Roasted Caesar Salad
with Salmon

77 Miso-Glazed Mahimahi
with Sesame–Sugar
Snap Peas

79 Cod in Parchment with
Tomatoes, Olives & Spinach

80 Creole Blackened Fish
with Herbed Rice & Peas

This classic French composed salad is made easy by using just one pan for cooking. Aioli is typically made with canola or vegetable oil because they impart very little flavor. Here, olive oil is added as well to create a luxurious aioli that works beautifully with this salad. Leftover aioli is delicious as a dip or on sandwiches.

AHI TUNA NIÇOISE SALAD WITH OLIVE OIL–DILL AIOLI

1 To prepare the aioli, in a food processor, combine the garlic and a big pinch of salt and pulse several times until the garlic is finely chopped. Add the egg and egg yolk and pulse to combine. In a liquid measuring cup, combine the canola oil and olive oil. With the machine running, slowly add a few drops of oil and then follow with a slow and steady stream of oil. Continue to purée until fully combined. Transfer to a bowl, stir in the dill, and adjust the seasoning with salt. Set aside at room temperature.

2 Preheat the oven to 450°F (230°C). Line a sheet pan with parchment paper.

3 In separate bowls, toss the potatoes, haricots verts, and cherry tomatoes each with 1 tablespoon of the olive oil and season with salt and pepper. Brush both sides of the tuna with the remaining 1 tablespoon olive oil and season both sides with salt and pepper.

4 Place the potatoes, cut side down, on one end of the prepared pan and roast until they are just beginning to soften, about 8 minutes. Place the haricots verts and cherry tomatoes in a single layer on the other end of the pan, leaving room for the tuna and olives, and roast for 5 minutes. Stir the vegetables and place the tuna and olives in a single layer on the pan. Continue roasting until the tuna is cooked through and the vegetables are fork-tender, about 10 minutes longer.

5 Arrange the potatoes, haricots verts, tomatoes, tuna, and olives on a large serving platter. Garnish with the eggs (if using) and the lemon wedges and serve right away with the aioli.

FOR THE OLIVE OIL–DILL AIOLI

1 clove garlic

Kosher salt

1 large egg plus 1 large egg yolk

1/2 cup (125 ml) canola oil

1/2 cup (125 ml) olive oil

2 tablespoons chopped fresh dill

3/4 lb (375 g) baby Dutch yellow or small red potatoes, halved

5 ounces (155 g) haricots verts

2 cups (12 oz/375 g) cherry tomatoes

4 tablespoons (60 ml) olive oil

Kosher salt and freshly ground pepper

2 ahi tuna steaks (about 1/2 lb/250 g each)

1 cup (5 oz/155 g) pitted Niçoise olives

3 hard-boiled large eggs, peeled and halved (optional)

1 lemon, cut into wedges

SERVES 4

A hot oven is imperative to ensure that these fries emerge golden and crisp but the shrimp don't overcook. If asparagus is not in season, make the fries with zucchini, squash, or mushrooms. If you can't find Meyer lemons, substitute any citrus.

GARLICKY SHRIMP WITH ASPARAGUS FRIES & MEYER LEMON AIOLI

FOR THE MEYER LEMON AIOLI

1 clove garlic

Kosher salt

1 large egg plus 1 large egg yolk

1 cup (250 ml) canola oil

Zest and juice of 1 Meyer lemon

FOR THE SHRIMP

1¼ lb (625 g) large shrimp, peeled and deveined, with tails intact

3 tablespoons olive oil

3 large cloves garlic, minced

1½ tablespoons Dijon mustard

1½ tablespoons lemon juice

Kosher salt and freshly ground pepper

FOR THE ASPARAGUS FRIES

½ cup (2½ oz/75 g) all-purpose flour

2 large eggs

1 cup (1½ oz/45 g) panko bread crumbs

¼ cup (1 oz/30 g) finely grated pecorino cheese

1 lb (500 g) asparagus

2 tablespoons chopped fresh flat-leaf parsley

SERVES 4

1 To prepare the aioli, in a food processor, combine the garlic and a big pinch of salt and pulse several times until the garlic is finely chopped. Add the egg and egg yolk and pulse to combine. With the machine running, slowly add a few drops of the canola oil and then follow with a slow and steady stream of oil. Continue to purée until fully combined. Transfer to a bowl, stir in the lemon zest and juice, and adjust the seasoning with salt. Set aside at room temperature.

2 Preheat the oven to 425°F (220°C). Lightly spray a sheet pan with nonstick cooking spray, line with aluminum foil, and spray again.

3 To prepare the shrimp, in a large bowl, toss together the shrimp, olive oil, garlic, mustard, and lemon juice, and season generously with salt and pepper. Set aside at room temperature.

4 To prepare the asparagus fries, place the flour in a bowl. In another bowl, whisk together the eggs and 1 tablespoon water. In a third bowl, stir together the panko and cheese, and season generously with salt and pepper. Cut or snap off the tough ends of the asparagus spears and discard. Dredge each asparagus spear in the flour, lightly coating on all sides, then dip into the egg mixture, letting the excess drip back into the bowl. Roll in the panko to coat completely. Place the asparagus in a single layer on one end of the prepared pan and season with salt. Place the shrimp on the other end of the pan.

5 Roast until the shrimp are opaque throughout and the fries are golden, 8–10 minutes. Garnish the shrimp with the parsley and serve right away with the fries and aioli.

While they seem like a fancy bistro dinner, mussels are economical and cook quickly. Here, they're roasted on a sheet pan with tomatoes, fennel, and bread crumbs for easy serving and cleanup. Be sure to discard any mussels that don't open during cooking, as this means they aren't safe to eat.

ROASTED MUSSELS WITH TOMATOES, FENNEL & BUTTERY BREAD CRUMBS

2 lb (1 kg) mussels, scrubbed and debearded

6 tablespoons (3 oz/90 g) unsalted butter, at room temperature

3 tomatoes, each cut into 6 wedges

2 fennel bulbs, trimmed, halved, and thinly sliced, fronds reserved

2 shallots, sliced

2 tablespoons olive oil

Kosher salt and freshly ground pepper

1 loaf crusty Italian bread

SERVES 4

1 Preheat the oven to 450°F (230°C).

2 Place the mussels on a sheet pan, spreading them out in a single layer. Cut 4 tablespoons (2 oz/60 g) of the butter into small pieces and sprinkle on top of the mussels. In a bowl, toss together the tomatoes, sliced fennel, shallots, and oil, and season with salt and pepper. Scatter the tomato mixture and the fennel fronds all around the mussels.

3 Cut two 1-inch (2.5-cm) slices from the loaf of bread. Pop them in the toaster on a low setting to dry them out slightly, then tear into small pieces.

Place in a food processor and pulse until fine crumbs form. Transfer the bread crumbs to a bowl and, using your hands, mix in the remaining 2 tablespoons butter. Season with salt and pepper and sprinkle the bread crumbs over the mussels and tomato mixture.

4 Roast until the mussels open and the bread crumbs are golden, 10–12 minutes. Discard any mussels that did not open. Serve right away, directly from the sheet pan so that no delicious juices are left behind, with the remaining bread for dipping.

Here, scallops, spinach, and lemon are combined to create a simple yet elegant dish that's fit for company. Use the larger sea scallops (rather than small bay scallops), which roast up beautifully in the oven. Baking citrus is a great way to brighten up a dish; the high temperature concentrates the sugars, resulting in extraordinary flavor.

ROASTED SCALLOPS WITH SPINACH & LEMONS

1 Preheat the oven to 325°F (165°C). Line a sheet pan with parchment paper.

2 Brush the lemon slices on one side with 1 tablespoon of the oil and season lightly with salt. Place in a single layer on the prepared pan, oiled side up, and roast for 20 minutes. Flip the lemons and continue roasting until the edges are browned, about 10 minutes longer. Transfer the lemons to a plate and set aside.

3 Raise the oven temperature to 400°F (200°C). In a large bowl, toss together the spinach and 2 tablespoons of the oil, and season with salt and pepper. Set aside.

4 In another large bowl, toss together the scallops and the remaining 2 tablespoons oil. Place the scallops on one end of the pan and brush the tops with the butter. Season generously with salt and pepper and roast for 7 minutes. Add the spinach and lemons to the other end of the pan and continue roasting until the scallops are just opaque throughout and the spinach is wilted, about 5 minutes longer. Serve right away.

2 lemons, sliced into ¹/₄-inch slices

5 tablespoons (80 ml) olive oil

Kosher salt and freshly ground pepper

2 bunches spinach, stemmed

20 sea scallops (about 1³/₄ lb/875 g total), side muscle removed

1 tablespoon unsalted butter, at room temperature

SERVES 4

Just a few ingredients—fish, white wine, and some aromatics—make an impressive yet easy dinner. Be sure to show off the whole roasted fish to your dinner companions before filleting it. Chimichurri is an Argentinean herb sauce that is best prepared just before serving so it will retain its vibrant green color.

WHOLE ROASTED FISH WITH FENNEL, LEMONS & CHIMICHURRI SAUCE

1 whole fish, such as bass, arctic char, or snapper (about 4 lb/2 kg)

3 tablespoons olive oil

Kosher salt and freshly ground black pepper

1 fennel bulb, trimmed, quartered, and sliced

2 lemons, sliced

1½ cups (375 ml) dry white wine

FOR THE CHIMICHURRI SAUCE

1 clove garlic

1½ teaspoons ground cumin

¼ teaspoon red pepper flakes

Kosher salt

1 cup (1 oz/30 g) packed fresh flat-leaf parsley leaves

½ cup (½ oz/15 g) packed fresh cilantro leaves

2 tablespoons red wine vinegar

6 tablespoons (90 ml) olive oil

SERVES 4–6

1 Preheat the oven to 400°F (200°C). Line a sheet pan with a piece of parchment paper or aluminum foil that is about 4 inches (10 cm) longer than the pan.

2 Make four 3-inch (7.5-cm) slits on both sides of the fish. Brush the fish inside and out with the oil, and season generously with salt and black pepper. Stuff the cavity with as much of the fennel and lemon slices as possible. Spread the rest out on the pan to create a bed and place the fish on top. Fold the foil up around the fish to create a border and pour the wine around the fish. Roast until the fish is opaque throughout, 30–35 minutes.

3 Meanwhile, prepare the chimichurri sauce: In a food processor or blender, combine the garlic, cumin, red pepper flakes, ½ teaspoon salt, the parsley, cilantro, and vinegar and pulse until finely chopped. With the machine running, add the oil in a slow, steady stream and process until fully incorporated. Adjust the seasoning with salt and set aside at room temperature.

4 Discard the lemon and fennel. Present the fish whole and then fillet it. Pass the chimichurri sauce at the table.

Paella cooks perfectly in the oven, yielding moist rice topped with flavorful seafood and chorizo. Be sure to use Spanish chorizo, which has been dried and cured, rather than fresh Mexican chorizo, for this dish. You can find jarred piquillo peppers in most grocery stores, but if they are unavailable, roasted red bell peppers will do the trick.

OVEN PAELLA WITH CHORIZO, CLAMS & SHRIMP

1 Preheat the oven to 350°F (180°C). Spray a sheet pan with nonstick cooking spray.

2 Spread the rice in a single layer on the prepared pan and toast in the oven for 5 minutes. In a large liquid measuring cup, stir together the broth, saffron, bay leaf, paprika, garlic, shallot, 1 teaspoon salt, and ¼ teaspoon pepper. Pour over the rice and stir to combine. Return the pan to the oven, carefully top with an inverted sheet pan or cover loosely with aluminum foil, and bake for 15 minutes. Remove from the oven and uncover the pan.

3 Stir the tomatoes, peppers, and chorizo into the rice. Using the back of a wooden spoon, spread the rice in an even layer and season with salt and pepper. In a bowl, toss together the shrimp and oil, and season with salt and pepper. Scatter the shrimp and clams all over the rice. Roast, uncovered, until the shrimp are opaque throughout and the clams open, about 12 minutes. Discard the bay leaf and any clams that did not open. Garnish with the parsley, drizzle with oil, and serve right away.

1 cup (7 oz/220 g) Arborio rice

2½ cups (625 ml) low-sodium chicken broth

1 teaspoon saffron, crumbled

1 bay leaf, torn in half

¾ teaspoon smoked paprika

2 cloves garlic, chopped

1 shallot, chopped

Kosher salt and freshly ground pepper

1 cup (6 oz/185 g) canned chopped tomatoes, drained

2 roasted piquillo peppers, halved and sliced

1 link Spanish cured chorizo (about 6 oz/185 g), cut into ¼-inch (6-mm) pieces

12 medium shrimp, peeled and deveined, with tails intact

2 teaspoons olive oil, plus more for drizzling

12 clams, scrubbed

2 tablespoons fresh flat-leaf parsley leaves

SERVES 4

Simple cooking from Southeast France is distinguished by fresh flavors and seasonal ingredients. Feel free to use any herbs you have on hand for this recipe, including dried ones. This dish is also wonderful served at room temperature for an outdoor buffet or a picnic.

SALMON PROVENÇAL WITH FINGERLING POTATOES & CHERRY TOMATOES

1 cup (6 oz/185 g) cherry tomatoes, preferably a mix of colors

2 tablespoons plus 2 teaspoons olive oil

Kosher salt and freshly ground pepper

4 center-cut wild salmon fillets (about 6 oz/185 g each)

2 tablespoons chopped fresh rosemary

2 tablespoons chopped fresh tarragon

1 lb (500 g) fingerling potatoes

1 tablespoon chopped fresh flat-leaf parsley

1 tablespoon fresh lemon juice

SERVES 4

1 Preheat the oven to 450°F (230°C). Line a sheet pan with parchment paper.

2 In a small bowl, toss together the cherry tomatoes and 1 teaspoon of the oil, and season with salt and pepper. Brush the salmon with 1 teaspoon of the oil and season with the rosemary, tarragon, salt, and pepper. Set aside.

3 Cut the potatoes in half lengthwise and cut any large ones in half crosswise as well. (You want them to be about the same size.) In a bowl, toss together the potatoes and the 2 tablespoons oil. Place, cut side down, on the prepared pan and season with salt and pepper. Roast for 8 minutes, then stir the potatoes. Place the tomatoes and salmon on the pan and continue roasting until the potatoes are fork-tender, the tomatoes just begin to burst, and the salmon is opaque throughout, 8–10 minutes longer.

4 Sprinkle the parsley over the vegetables and pour the lemon juice over the salmon. Serve right away.

Don't knock it until you've tried it—roasted lettuce adds a smoky flavor that complements the deep salty flavors in a Caesar salad dressing. The crisp, compact leaves from the hearts of romaine work best under heat to avoid a limp salad. For a change, swap out the salmon for grilled shrimp, chicken, or tofu.

ROASTED CAESAR SALAD WITH SALMON

4 center-cut wild salmon fillets (about 6 oz/185 g each)

3 tablespoons olive oil

Salt and freshly ground pepper

3 anchovies in olive oil

1 clove garlic

1 teaspoon dried mustard

Juice of 1 lemon

2 hearts of romaine

¼ cup (1 oz/30 g) freshly grated Parmesan cheese

SERVES 4–6

1 Preheat the oven to 425°F (220°C). Line a sheet pan with parchment paper.

2 Place the salmon on one end of the prepared pan. Brush the salmon with 1 tablespoon of the oil and season with salt and pepper. Roast for 5 minutes.

3 Finely chop the anchovies and garlic on a cutting board and sprinkle with ½ teaspoon salt. Use the side of your knife to make a paste and transfer to a mixing bowl. Stir in the mustard and the lemon juice. Whisk in the remaining 2 tablespoons olive oil and season to taste with more salt and pepper.

4 Place the hearts of Romaine on the other end of the sheet pan. Brush with a good amount of the dressing and transfer to the oven. Roast just until the salmon is opaque throughout and the top of the lettuce begins to char, 7–10 minutes. Remove the pan from the oven. Sprinkle the lettuce with the Parmesan cheese.

5 Chop the lettuce into 1-inch (2.5-cm) pieces and pile it onto 4 plates. Top each plate with a piece of salmon and drizzle with the remaining dressing. Serve right away.

Several varieties of miso paste are available, including white, yellow, and red. Use white miso for this recipe, as its sweet, mellow taste won't overpower the fish, which is broiled so that the glaze will caramelize well. You can substitute other types of fish in this dish, such as halibut, swordfish, bass, tuna, or bluefish.

MISO-GLAZED MAHIMAHI WITH SESAME-SUGAR SNAP PEAS

1 In a large bowl, whisk together the miso, mirin, vinegar, soy sauce, and brown sugar. Add the fish and turn to coat. Cover and refrigerate for at least 2 hours or up to 6 hours, turning the fish once.

2 Position a rack 4–6 inches (10–15 cm) from the heat source and preheat the broiler. Line a sheet pan with parchment paper

3 In a bowl, toss together the sugar snap peas and oil, and season with salt. Set aside.

4 Remove the fish from the marinade and place on the prepared pan. Broil for 4 minutes. Place the snap peas in a single layer on the pan and continue broiling until the fish is opaque throughout and the snap peas are fork-tender, 5–7 minutes longer.

5 Sprinkle the sesame seeds over the snap peas and serve right away.

¼ cup (2 oz/60 g) white miso

2 tablespoons mirin

2 tablespoons rice vinegar

2 tablespoons low-sodium soy sauce

2 tablespoons firmly packed brown sugar

4 mahimahi fillets (about ⅓ lb/155 g) each

1 lb (500 g) sugar snap peas, trimmed

1½ teaspoons dark sesame oil

Kosher salt

1 tablespoon toasted sesame seeds

SERVES 4

Baking *en papillote*, or in parchment paper, is a terrific way to cook healthy and unfussy food, and you need very little fat to ensure juicy results. You can assemble the packets several hours in advance and refrigerate, then bake just before serving.

COD IN PARCHMENT WITH TOMATOES, OLIVES & SPINACH

1 Preheat the oven to 375°F (190°C). Cut parchment paper into four 10-inch (25-cm) squares and place on a work surface.

2 Place one-fourth of the spinach in the center of each square. Drizzle 2 tablespoons of the oil over the spinach and season with salt and pepper. Place a fish fillet on each pile of spinach and top with the tomatoes, olives, and rosemary, dividing evenly. Drizzle with the remaining 2 tablespoons oil, season with salt and pepper, and sprinkle with the lemon juice.

3 Bring the front and back sides of the parchment paper together to meet in the center, fold them over, and then tuck the sides underneath the packets. Place on a sheet pan and bake until the fish is opaque throughout, about 15 minutes. Carefully open the packets (steam will be trapped inside) and serve right away.

4 cups (4 oz/125 g) packed baby spinach

4 tablespoons (60 ml) olive oil

Kosher salt and freshly ground pepper

4 cod fillets (about 6 oz/ 185 g each)

3 Roma tomatoes, chopped

1/2 cup (2 1/2 oz/75 g) cured black olives, pitted and halved

1 tablespoon dried rosemary

Juice of 1/2 lemon

SERVES 4

There are many versions of spice mixtures for Creole cooking, so feel free to experiment with other combinations. Leftover spices are fantastic roasted with potatoes and olive oil. For a delicious variation, wrap the fish and rice in warm tortillas and serve with a fruit salsa. Because this dish packs some heat, offer ice-cold beer or lemonade alongside.

CREOLE BLACKENED FISH WITH HERBED RICE & PEAS

1 cup (7 oz/220 g) long-grain white rice

2¹/₂ cups (625 ml) low-sodium chicken or vegetable broth

1 shallot, finely chopped

2 cloves garlic, finely chopped

4 flaky white fish fillets, such as tilapia, catfish, snapper, or trout (about 6 oz/185 g each)

Kosher salt and freshly ground black pepper

1¹/₂ teaspoons garlic powder

1¹/₂ teaspoons onion powder

1¹/₂ teaspoons dried oregano

1¹/₂ teaspoons paprika

³/₄ teaspoon dried thyme

¹/₄ teaspoon cayenne pepper

¹/₂ cup (2¹/₂ oz/75 g) peas

¹/₄ cup (¹/₂ oz/15 g) fresh oregano leaves, chopped

¹/₄ cup (¹/₂ oz/15 g) fresh flat-leaf parsley leaves, chopped

2 tablespoons olive oil

1 lemon, cut into wedges

SERVES 4

1 Preheat the oven to 350°F (180°C). Spray a sheet pan with nonstick cooking spray.

2 Spread the rice in a single layer on the prepared pan and toast in the oven for 5 minutes. In a large liquid measuring cup, stir together the broth, shallot, and garlic. Pour over the rice and stir to combine. Cover the pan tightly with aluminum foil and bake for 15 minutes. Remove from the oven and uncover the pan.

3 Season the fish with salt. In a small bowl, stir together the garlic powder, onion powder, dried oregano, paprika, thyme, cayenne, and ¹/₄ teaspoon black pepper. Coat one side of each fillet with the spice mixture. Set aside.

4 Raise the oven temperature to 375°F (190°C).

5 Stir the peas, fresh oregano, and parsley into the rice and season well with salt and black pepper. Using a wooden spoon, create 4 pockets in the rice for the fish and place a fillet in each one. Roast, uncovered, until the fish is opaque throughout and the rice is tender, about 10 minutes. Drizzle the fish and rice with the oil and serve right away with lemon wedges.

vegetables

87 White Pizza with Potatoes & Sun-Dried Tomatoes

90 Stuffed Eggplant Three Ways

92 Cauliflower Steaks with Capers, Anchovies & Winter Greens

95 Roasted Corn, Asparagus & Spring Onion Salad with Fresh Mozzarella

96 Portobello Mushroom Parmesan with Herbed Summer Squash

97 Gingery Asian Eggplant with Tofu & Green Beans

98 Lemony Tofu & Vegetable Kebabs with Roasted Poblano Sauce

101 Brussels Sprouts & Potato Hash with Baked Eggs

102 Loaded Baked Potatoes with Pancetta, Broccoli & Cheddar Cheese

103 Mushroom & Gruyère Tart with Hazelnut Haricots Verts

105 Vegetable Pizza Tarts

The key to a crispy pizza crust is to let the oven preheat for a long time so it's really, really hot. A white pizza, made without red sauce, lends itself well to vegetable toppings and simple ingredients. If you are short on time, use prepared pizza dough.

WHITE PIZZA WITH POTATOES & SUN-DRIED TOMATOES

1 To prepare the pizza dough, in a food processor, combine the flours, yeast, sugar, and 1 tablespoon salt. With the machine running, add the warm water and oil in a steady stream and then pulse until the dough comes together in a rough mass, about 12 seconds. If the dough does not form into a ball, sprinkle with 1–2 teaspoons water and pulse again until a rough mass forms. Let the dough rest for 5–10 minutes, then process again until it is tacky to the touch but not sticky, 25–30 seconds.

2 Turn the dough out onto a lightly floured work surface and form into a smooth ball. Transfer to an oiled bowl and turn to coat all sides. Cover the bowl with plastic wrap and let the dough rise in a warm place until doubled in bulk, about 1½ hours. Divide the dough in half, transfer one half to a lock-top plastic bag, and freeze for up to 2 months.

3 Preheat the oven to 450°F (230°C). Once the oven has reached 450°F (230°C), let the oven continue to heat for 15 minutes longer, without opening the door. Line a sheet pan with parchment paper.

4 On a floured work surface, roll out the remaining dough into a 10-by-13-inch (25-by-33-cm) rectangle. If the dough springs back, let it rest for 10 minutes before continuing to roll it out. Transfer the dough to the prepared pan and brush with 1 tablespoon of the oil.

5 Sprinkle the dough with the mozzarella, leaving a 1-inch (2.5-cm) border. In a bowl, stir together the ricotta, Parmesan, and 1 tablespoon of the oil. Dollop the cheese mixture by the tablespoonful over the mozzarella.

6 Using a mandoline or a sharp knife, slice the potatoes as thinly as possible. Transfer to a bowl and toss with the remaining 1 tablespoon oil. Arrange the potatoes in a single layer over the pizza so they will cook evenly. Season the pizza with salt and pepper.

7 Bake until the crust is golden and the cheese is melted, about 14 minutes. Remove the pizza from the oven. Scatter the sun-dried tomatoes and basil on top and drizzle with oil. Cut into slices and serve right away.

FOR THE PIZZA DOUGH

3½ cups (17½ oz/545 g) all-purpose flour, plus more for dusting

¼ cup (1½ oz/45 g) whole-wheat flour

1 package (2½ teaspoons) quick-rise yeast

1 tablespoon sugar

Kosher salt

1¼ cups (310 ml) warm water, plus more as needed

Olive oil as needed

3 tablespoons olive oil, plus more for drizzling

1 cup (4 oz/125 g) shredded mozzarella cheese

1 cup (8 oz/250 g) whole-milk ricotta cheese

¼ cup (1 oz/30 g) grated Parmesan cheese

2 small red potatoes, (about ¼ lb/125 g total), unpeeled

Kosher salt and freshly ground pepper

⅓ cup (2 oz/60 g) drained oil-packed sun-dried tomatoes

¼ cup (¼ oz/7 g) fresh basil leaves, torn

SERVES 2–4

What follows is a master recipe for roasting eggplant, an ideal and versatile vegetable for sheet-pan roasting. Fill them with one of the three savory mixtures suggested here, or prepare your own favorite stuffing, or mix and match. Choose fresh eggplants that are shiny, smooth, and firm but not hard.

STUFFED EGGPLANT THREE WAYS

6 small eggplants (about 2 lb/1 kg total), any variety

2 tablespoons olive oil

Kosher salt and freshly ground pepper

CAPRESE WITH ARTICHOKES & BASIL

1¹/₂ cups (9 oz/280 g) cherry tomatoes, quartered

¹/₂ lb (250 g) bocconcini (fresh mozzarella cheese balls), drained and halved

1¹/₄ cups (8 oz/250 g) artichoke hearts, drained well and chopped

¹/₄ cup (¹/₄ oz/7 g) packed fresh basil leaves, chopped, plus more for garnish

3 tablespoons olive oil

1 tablespoon balsamic vinegar

Kosher salt and freshly ground pepper

1 Preheat the oven to 400°F (200°C). Line a sheet pan with parchment paper.

2 Cut the top off each eggplant and cut in half lengthwise. Using a paring knife, remove the flesh, leaving a ¹/₄-inch (6-mm) shell, and cut the flesh into ¹/₄-inch (6-mm) cubes.

3 Brush the eggplant halves inside and out with 1 tablespoon of the oil and season with salt and pepper. Place, cut side up, on the prepared pan. In a bowl, toss together the eggplant cubes and the remaining 2 tablespoons oil, and season with salt and pepper. Place on the prepared pan. Roast until fork-tender, 20–25 minutes. Follow the instructions for preparing one or more of the fillings; each recipe will fill 6 eggplants.

CAPRESE WITH ARTICHOKES & BASIL

In a large bowl, stir together the roasted eggplant cubes, the cherry tomatoes, bocconcini, artichoke hearts, basil, oil, and vinegar, and season with salt and pepper. Fill the eggplant cavities so they are piled high, and roast until warm throughout and cheese begins to melt, about 10 minutes. Garnish the eggplant halves with basil and serve right away.

FARRO WITH FRESH HERB PISTOU & YOGURT SAUCE

In a large bowl, stir together the roasted eggplant cubes, the farro, 2 tablespoons of the oil, the cumin, and cinnamon, and season with salt and pepper. Fill the eggplant cavities so they are piled high, and roast until warmed throughout, about 10 minutes.

Meanwhile, make the pistou: In a small bowl, stir together the garlic, parsley, mint, the remaining 1 1/2 tablespoons oil, and the lemon zest, and season with salt and pepper. In another small bowl, stir together the yogurt and lemon juice, and season with salt and pepper.

Dollop the pistou over the eggplant halves, drizzle with the yogurt sauce, and serve right away.

KALE & RICOTTA WITH ALMONDS

Spread the ricotta on the bottom of the eggplant cavities. In a large bowl, stir together the roasted eggplant cubes, the kale, garlic, oil, and vinegar, and season with salt and pepper. Fill the eggplant cavities so they are piled high and scatter the almonds on top. Roast until the kale wilts and filling is warmed throughout, about 10 minutes. Serve right away.

FARRO WITH FRESH HERB PISTOU & YOGURT SAUCE

2 cups (10 oz/315 g) cooked farro or other grain, such as brown rice, quinoa, or couscous

3 1/2 tablespoons olive oil

2 teaspoons ground cumin

1 teaspoon ground cinnamon

Kosher salt and freshly ground pepper

1 clove garlic, pressed or minced

1/2 cup (1/2 oz/15 g) fresh flat-leaf parsley leaves, finely chopped

1/4 cup (1/4 oz/7 g) fresh mint leaves, finely chopped

Zest and juice of 1 lemon

1 cup (8 oz/250 g) plain whole-milk yogurt

KALE & RICOTTA WITH ALMONDS

1/2 cup (4 oz/125 g) whole-milk ricotta cheese

3 cups (6 oz/180 g) packed baby kale

2 cloves garlic, pressed or minced

3 tablespoons olive oil

1 tablespoon balsamic vinegar

Kosher salt and freshly ground pepper

3 tablespoons slivered almonds

SERVES 4

Cauliflower is a meaty vegetable that makes a substantial base for a satisfying meal. When you slice the cauliflower into steaks, it's inevitable that some florets will break free. Just place them on the pan as well. Add the greens in batches because they will not all fit on the pan at once (they shrink considerably as they cook).

CAULIFLOWER STEAKS WITH CAPERS, ANCHOVIES & WINTER GREENS

1 large head cauliflower, bottom of head trimmed but stem left intact

8 tablespoons (125 ml) olive oil, plus more for drizzling

3 cloves garlic, chopped

4 anchovy fillets in olive oil, chopped

1/4 cup (2 oz/60 g) capers

Kosher salt and freshly ground pepper

1 bunch kale, thick stems removed, cut into 2-inch (5-cm) slices

1 bunch chard, thick stems removed, cut into 2-inch (5-cm) slices

Juice of 1/2 lemon

1/4 cup (1 1/2 oz/45 g) dried cherries

SERVES 2–4

1 Preheat the oven to 400°F (200°C). Line a sheet pan with aluminum foil.

2 Place the cauliflower, stem side down, on a cutting board and cut into 3/4-inch (2-cm) slices that include the stem. Brush both sides of the slices with 2 tablespoons of the oil and place in a single layer on one end of the prepared pan. In a bowl, stir together 3 tablespoons of the oil, the garlic, anchovies, and capers. Brush the mixture over the tops of the cauliflower and season with salt and pepper. Roast until the cauliflower begins to soften, about 10 minutes.

3 In a large bowl, toss together the kale, chard, and the remaining 3 tablespoons oil. Place half of the greens on the other end of the pan and season

with salt and pepper. Roast until the greens are beginning to soften, about 6 minutes. Place the remaining greens on top of the softened greens and toss to combine. Continue roasting until the cauliflower is golden and fork-tender and the greens are wilted, 8–10 minutes longer.

4 Toss the greens with the lemon juice and dried cherries. Using a spatula, carefully transfer the cauliflower steaks to plates, drizzle with oil, and serve right away with the greens on the side.

This beautiful dinner salad can be served warm or at room temperature and is perfect served with a fresh baguette and a crisp white wine. Always buy corn completely enclosed in the husk, as the kernels begin to lose their sweetness after shucking. For optimal flavor, serve the fresh mozzarella at room temperature.

ROASTED CORN, ASPARAGUS & SPRING ONION SALAD WITH FRESH MOZZARELLA

1 Preheat the oven to 425°F (220°C). Line a sheet pan with aluminum foil.

2 In a bowl, toss together the onions and 2 tablespoons of the oil, and season with salt and pepper. Place the onions in a single layer on one end of the prepared pan. Brush the corn with 1 tablespoon of the oil and season with salt and pepper. Place on the pan in a single layer, leaving room for the asparagus, and roast for 15 minutes.

3 In a bowl, toss together the asparagus, 1 tablespoon of the oil, and 2 teaspoons of the vinegar. Place the asparagus in a single layer on the pan and season with salt and pepper. Continue roasting until the vegetables are fork-tender, about 10 minutes longer.

4 When the corn is cool enough to handle, cut the kernels from the cobs onto the sheet pan. Toss together the corn, onions, and asparagus directly on the pan. Divide the vegetables among 4 plates.

5 In a bowl, toss together the bocconcini and the remaining 2 tablespoons oil and 2 teaspoons vinegar. Nestle the bocconcini into the salads and garnish with the radishes. Drizzle with oil, season with salt and pepper, and serve.

4 purple spring onions, trimmed and quartered

6 tablespoons (90 ml) olive oil, plus more for drizzling

Kosher salt and freshly ground pepper

4 ears of corn, husks and silks removed

1 lb (500 g) asparagus, trimmed

4 teaspoons balsamic vinegar

$^1/_2$ lb (250 g) bocconcini (fresh mozzarella cheese balls), drained, at room temperature

3 radishes, trimmed, halved, and thinly sliced

SERVES 4

Individual Parmesans are easy to prepare and impressive to serve. Here, they're made with portobello mushrooms, which are so earthy and satisfying that you'll forget about meat or pasta altogether. Eggplant can be used in place of the mushroom base. Clean the mushrooms by wiping them with a paper towel.

PORTOBELLO MUSHROOM PARMESAN WITH HERBED SUMMER SQUASH

4 portobello mushrooms, brushed clean and stemmed

4 tablespoons (60 ml) olive oil

Kosher salt and freshly ground pepper

2 small yellow squash, halved lengthwise and cut into ½-inch (12-mm) pieces

2 small zucchini, halved lengthwise and cut into ½-inch (12-mm) pieces

1½ tablespoons fresh oregano leaves, chopped

1 can (15 oz/470 g) diced fire-roasted tomatoes with juices

3 tablespoons chopped fresh basil

¼ lb (125 g) fresh mozzarella cheese, sliced

¼ cup (1 oz/30 g) grated Parmesan cheese

½ cup (1 oz/30 g) fresh bread crumbs

1½ tablespoons unsalted butter, at room temperature

SERVES 4

1 Preheat the oven to 400°F (200°C). Line a sheet pan with aluminum foil.

2 Brush the mushrooms on both sides with 2 tablespoons of the oil and season with salt and pepper. Place the mushrooms, stem side up, on one side of the prepared pan. In a bowl, toss together the squash, zucchini, oregano, and the remaining 2 tablespoons oil, and season generously with salt and pepper. Place in a single layer on the other side of the pan and roast just until the vegetables begin to soften, about 7 minutes.

3 Meanwhile, in a food processor or blender, purée the tomatoes with their juices until smooth. Transfer to a bowl and stir in the basil. Fill the mushroom caps with the tomato mixture, dividing evenly. Top with the mozzarella and Parmesan. In a small bowl, stir together the bread crumbs and butter and sprinkle over the cheese. Season with salt and pepper.

4 Continue roasting just until the cheese melts, the bread crumbs are golden, and the squash and zucchini are fork-tender, 10–12 minutes longer. Serve right away.

This oven "stir-fry" makes a delicious and healthy Asian dinner. The tofu is pressed between paper towels to soak up as much moisture as possible. That way, it will absorb more of the marinade and caramelize in the oven. Serve over white or brown rice, if desired.

GINGERY ASIAN EGGPLANT WITH TOFU & GREEN BEANS

1 Cut the tofu in half horizontally. Place 3 paper towels on a plate and lay the tofu slices in a single layer on the towels. Top with 3 more paper towels and another plate. Use something heavy, such as a pot, to weigh down the top plate. Let stand for 5 minutes. Repeat the process with fresh paper towels. Cut the tofu into ³/₄-inch (2-cm) cubes.

2 Preheat the oven to 400°F (200°C). Line a sheet pan with aluminum foil.

3 In a large bowl, stir together the soy sauce, canola oil, sesame oil, vinegar, ginger, garlic, and chili oil (if using). Add the tofu, eggplant, and green beans and toss to combine. Let stand at room temperature for 20 minutes, stirring a few times.

4 Place the tofu and vegetables in a single layer on the prepared pan. Roast, stirring halfway through cooking, until the tofu is caramelized on the edges and the vegetables are fork-tender, about 30 minutes. Serve right away.

14 oz (440 g) extra-firm tofu, drained

¹/₃ cup (80 ml) low-sodium soy sauce

¹/₄ cup (60 ml) canola or vegetable oil

2 tablespoons dark sesame oil

2 tablespoons rice wine vinegar

1¹/₂-inch (4-cm) piece fresh ginger, peeled and grated

2 cloves garlic, chopped

¹/₄ teaspoon chili oil (optional)

3 Asian eggplants (1 lb/ 500 g total), cut into 1-inch (2.5-cm) pieces

¹/₂ lb (250 g) green beans, trimmed

SERVES 4

This nutritious combination of protein-packed tofu and fresh vegetables gets bright flavor from a creamy poblano sauce. Poblanos are a relatively mild chile, but like all chiles, they don't reveal how hot they will be until you cut into them. Most of the heat is found in the membrane that attaches the seeds to the chile.

LEMONY TOFU & VEGETABLE KEBABS WITH ROASTED POBLANO SAUCE

1 lb (500 g) extra-firm tofu, drained

Juice of 2 lemons

1½ teaspoons ground cumin

Kosher salt and freshly ground pepper

½ cup (125 ml) olive oil

2 Asian eggplants, halved lengthwise and cut into 1-inch (2.5-cm) pieces

2 zucchini, halved lengthwise and cut into 1-inch (2.5-cm) pieces

16 small cherry tomatoes

2 poblano chiles, halved lengthwise, seeded, and deribbed

2 shallots, halved lengthwise

½ cup (½ oz/15 g) fresh cilantro leaves

1 clove garlic

½ cup (4 oz/125 g) sour cream

Juice of 1 lime

SERVES 4

1 If using wooden skewers, soak 8–10 skewers in water for at least 30 minutes.

2 Cut the tofu in half horizontally. Place 3 paper towels on a plate and lay the tofu slices in a single layer on the towels. Top with 3 more paper towels and another plate. Use something heavy, such as a pot, to weigh down the top plate. Let stand for 5 minutes. Repeat the process with fresh paper towels. Cut the tofu into 1-inch (2.5-cm) cubes.

3 Preheat the oven to 400°F (200°C). Line a sheet pan with aluminum foil.

4 In a large bowl, stir together the lemon juice, cumin, 1 teaspoon salt, ½ teaspoon pepper, and the oil. Add the tofu, eggplant, zucchini, and cherry tomatoes and toss to combine. Let stand at room temperature for 15 minutes, stirring twice.

5 Thread the tofu and vegetables onto the skewers, alternating as you go, and place on one end of the prepared pan. Place the poblano chiles and shallots, cut side down, on the other end of the pan. Roast for 15 minutes, then flip the skewers and transfer the chiles and shallots to a plate. Continue roasting the skewers until the vegetables are fork-tender, 10–12 minutes longer. Remove the pan from the oven and tent loosely with foil.

6 In a food processor or blender, combine the chiles, shallots, cilantro, and garlic and pulse until finely chopped. Scrape down the sides of the bowl. Add the sour cream and lime juice and process until smooth. Transfer to a bowl and season with salt.

7 Drizzle the skewers with the poblano sauce and serve right away.

Breakfast for dinner always gets high praise from diners, and you can feel good about this dish because it's loaded with vegetables and high-protein eggs. Keep in mind that the eggs will continue to cook from the residual heat after you remove the pan from the oven.

BRUSSELS SPROUTS & POTATO HASH WITH BAKED EGGS

1 Preheat the oven to 425°F (220°C). Line a sheet pan with aluminum foil.

2 Trim the ends off the brussels sprouts, halve them lengthwise, and then coarsely chop into small dice. They will fall apart and this is okay. Transfer the brussels sprouts to a large bowl. Add the potatoes, thyme, shallots, garlic, and oil and stir to combine. Place the vegetables in a single layer on the prepared pan and season generously with salt and pepper. Roast for 15 minutes, then stir the vegetables and spread them out in a single layer again. Drizzle with more oil if they seem dry. Continue roasting until the vegetables are golden and fork-tender, about 15 minutes longer.

3 Using a spoon, make 8 small wells for the eggs in the vegetables. Crack 1 egg into each well and season with salt and pepper. Bake until the eggs are mostly set, 6–8 minutes.

4 To serve, carefully scoop 2 eggs and some of the hash into each of 4 bowls. Serve right away with hot sauce, if using.

1¹/₄ lb (625 g) brussels sprouts

2 russet potatoes, unpeeled, cut into ¹/₄-inch (6-mm) pieces

3 tablespoons fresh thyme leaves, roughly chopped

2 shallots, halved and sliced

2 cloves garlic, chopped

¹/₂ cup (125 ml) olive oil, plus more as needed

Kosher salt and freshly ground pepper

8 large eggs

Hot sauce, for serving (optional)

SERVES 4

This simple yet satisfying dinner is easy and appealing to all ages. While white potatoes tend to get a bad rap, they are high in fiber and low in fat. Serve this meal family-style and let diners fill their own potatoes. For a variation, try sweet potatoes with bacon, spinach, Gruyère cheese, and a lemony sour cream.

LOADED BAKED POTATOES WITH PANCETTA, BROCCOLI & CHEDDAR CHEESE

4 russet potatoes (about 3 lb/1.5 kg total)

5 oz (155 g) pancetta, chopped

¾ lb (375 g) broccoli, cut into small florets

2 tablespoons olive oil

Kosher salt and freshly ground pepper

½ cup (4 oz/125 g) sour cream

3 tablespoons chopped fresh chives

1 tablespoon fresh lemon juice

½ cup (2 oz/60 g) shredded Cheddar cheese

SERVES 4

1 Preheat the oven to 450°F (230°C). Lightly spray a baking sheet with nonstick cooking spray, cover with aluminum foil, and spray again.

2 Place the potatoes on one side of the prepared pan, prick them several times with a fork, and bake for 40 minutes. Place the pancetta on the other side of the pan, leaving room for the broccoli, and bake until the fat begins to render, about 10 minutes.

3 In a bowl, toss together the broccoli and oil, and season with salt and pepper. Place the broccoli on the pan, stir the pancetta, and continue baking until the pancetta is crispy and the potatoes and broccoli are fork-tender, 15–20 minutes longer.

4 In a small bowl, stir together the sour cream, chives, and lemon juice, and season with salt and pepper.

5 Cut the potatoes lengthwise and fill with the pancetta, broccoli, and cheese. Pass the chive sour cream at the table.

The wonderful thing about tarts is that the toppings are endless, and the tarts can be cooked in advance and served at room temperature or reheated in the oven. Either way, they make a deliciously light dinner, and leftovers are equally as tasty for lunch the next day.

MUSHROOM & GRUYÈRE TART WITH HAZELNUT HARICOTS VERTS

1 Preheat the oven to 400°F (200°C). Line a sheet pan with parchment paper.

2 On a lightly floured work surface, roll out the puff pastry into a 12½-by-15-inch (32-by-38-cm) rectangle. Fold into thirds, transfer to the prepared pan, and unfold, positioning the dough so there will be room for the haricots verts on the pan. Fold over about 1 inch (2.5 cm) of each side of the dough to create a border.

3 Sprinkle the dough with the cheese, leaving the borders uncovered. In a bowl, toss together the leeks, mushrooms, and 3 tablespoons of the oil, and season with salt and pepper.

Spread the mixture over the cheese. Brush the borders with the egg mixture. Bake for 10 minutes.

4 In a bowl, toss together the haricots verts and the remaining 1½ tablespoons oil, and season with salt and pepper. Place in a single layer on the pan next to the tart. Continue baking until the tart is golden brown and the haricots verts are fork-tender, about 15 minutes longer. During the last 5 minutes of cooking, sprinkle the hazelnuts over the haricots verts.

5 Let the tart cool slightly, then cut into slices and serve the haricots verts on the side.

All-purpose flour, for dusting

1 sheet frozen puff pastry (half of a 17.3-oz/490-g package), thawed

5 ounces (155 g) Gruyère cheese, shredded

2 leeks, trimmed, halved lengthwise, white and pale parts thinly sliced

¼ lb (125 g) white mushrooms, brushed clean and thinly sliced

4½ tablespoons (70 ml) olive oil

Kosher salt and freshly ground pepper

1 large egg beaten with 1 tablespoon water

¾ lb (375 g) haricots verts, trimmed

¼ cup (1¼ oz/40 g) hazelnuts, roughly chopped

SERVES 2–4

To make your own pesto, in a food processor, purée 2 cups (2 oz/60 g) fresh basil leaves, 2 cloves garlic, and ¼ cup (1¼ oz/40 g) toasted pine nuts. Slowly add ½ cup (125 ml) olive oil, then stir in ½ cup (2 oz/60 g) grated Parmesan cheese and salt, to taste. Experiment with different herbs and nuts; just keep the same quantities.

VEGETABLE PIZZA TARTS

1 Preheat the oven to 425°F (220°C). Line a sheet pan with parchment paper.

2 On a lightly floured work surface, roll out 1 puff pastry sheet into a 12-inch (30-cm) square and cut in half. Fold over about ¼ inch (6 mm) of each side of the dough to create a border and transfer to one end of the prepared pan. Repeat with the remaining dough half and then with the second puff pastry sheet, positioning the tart shells an equal distance apart on the pan.

3 To prepare the bell pepper, red onion, and feta tart, in a small bowl, stir together the tomato purée, garlic, and oregano, and season with salt and pepper. Spread the tomato sauce onto 2 of the tart shells and sprinkle with the feta cheese. In another small bowl,

toss the onion with the oil and vinegar. Scatter the onion and the bell pepper on top of the feta.

4 To prepare the mozzarella, pesto, and mushroom tart, spread the pesto onto the remaining 2 tart shells and cover with the mozzarella cheese and tomato slices. In a small bowl, toss the mushrooms with the oil and scatter over the tarts. Season all of the tarts with salt and pepper.

5 Bake until the tarts are golden brown, about 20 minutes. Let the tarts stand at room temperature.

6 Sprinkle the pesto tarts with the basil. Cut each tart into rectangles, and serve.

All-purpose flour, for dusting

2 sheets frozen puff pastry (17.3-oz/490-g package), thawed

FOR THE BELL PEPPER, RED ONION & FETA TART

1 cup (8 oz/250 g) tomato purée

1 large clove garlic, minced

1 teaspoon dried oregano

Kosher salt and freshly ground pepper

1 cup (5 oz/155 g) crumbled feta cheese

½ cup (2 oz/60 g) thinly sliced red onion

1 tablespoon olive oil

2 teaspoons balsamic vinegar

1 red bell pepper, roasted, seeded, and thinly sliced

FOR THE MOZZARELLA, PESTO & MUSHROOM TART

1 cup (250 ml) basil pesto (see note above)

1 cup (4 oz/125 g) shredded mozzarella cheese

1 Roma tomato, thinly sliced

3 white mushrooms, brushed clean and thinly sliced

1 tablespoon olive oil

3 tablespoons chopped fresh basil

SERVES 4–6

INDEX

A

Ahi Tuna Niçoise Salad with
Olive Oil–Dill Aioli, 65

Anchovies, Capers & Winter Greens,
Cauliflower Steaks with, 92

Apricots, Red Cabbage & Blue Cheese,
Pork Chops with, 46

Artichokes
Spiced Lamb Patties with
Orange-Thyme Tapenade
& Baby Artichokes, 54
Stuffed Eggplant Three Ways, 90–91

Arugula
Porchetta with Wilted Arugula
& Warm Dates, 51
Roasted Chicken with Giant Croutons,
Sweet Potatoes & Arugula, 21

Asparagus
Chicken Schnitzel with Asparagus, 28
Garlicky Shrimp with Asparagus Fries
& Meyer Lemon Aioli, 64
Roasted Corn, Asparagus & Spring
Onion Salad with Fresh
Mozzarella, 95

B

Bangers & Smashed Potatoes with
Whole-Grain Dijonnaise, 40

Banh Mi, Vietnamese Turkey Meatball
& Hoisin Eggplant, 34

Beans
Ahi Tuna Niçoise Salad with
Olive Oil–Dill Aioli, 65
Asian Five-Spice Pork Tenderloin with
Honey-Roasted Edamame, 48
Gingery Asian Eggplant with
Tofu & Green Beans, 97
Mushroom & Gruyère Tart with
Hazelnut Haricots Verts, 103

Beef
Bangers & Smashed Potatoes with
Whole-Grain Dijonnaise, 40
Herb-Crusted Beef Tenderloin
with Ratatouille, 43

Meat Loaf with Roasted Mushrooms
& Smashed Butternut Squash, 35

Mexican Stuffed Peppers with
Chipotle Sweet Potatoes, 33

Oven Ribs with Mop Sauce &
Pecorino-Jalapeño-Dusted Corn, 38

Roasted Red Pepper, Spinach
& Asiago Stuffed Flank Steak
with Brown Sugared Carrots, 37

Skirt Steak with Smoky
Compound Butter & Blistered
Shishito Peppers, 44

Standing Rib Roast with Rosemary
Root Vegetables & Horseradish
Sauce, 45

Zucchini Bolognese al Forno, 41

Bread & toasts
Bruschetta with Chili-Spiced
Leg of Lamb & Caramelized
Red Onions, 58
Roasted Chicken with Giant Croutons,
Sweet Potatoes & Arugula, 21
Roasted Mussels with Tomatoes,
Fennel & Buttery Bread Crumbs, 68

Broccoli
Loaded Baked Potatoes with Pancetta,
Broccoli & Cheddar Cheese, 102
Spicy Asian Chicken Drumettes with
Broccoli & Spiced Walnuts, 30

Broccoli Rabe, Pork & Green Chile
Empanadas with, 55

Bruschetta with Chili-Spiced Leg of
Lamb & Caramelized Red Onions, 58

Brussels sprouts
Brussels Sprouts & Potato Hash
with Baked Eggs, 101
Pork Shoulder with Brussels Sprouts
& Roasted Tomato Chermoula, 49

C

Cabbage, Red, Apricots & Blue Cheese,
Pork Chops with, 46

Capers, Anchovies & Winter Greens,
Cauliflower Steaks with, 92

Carrots, Brown Sugared, Roasted
Red Pepper, Spinach & Asiago
Stuffed Flank Steak with, 37

Cauliflower
Cauliflower Steaks with Capers,
Anchovies & Winter Greens, 92
Chicken Tikka Masala with Roasted
Cauliflower & Red Onion, 25

Cheese
Loaded Baked Potatoes with
Pancetta, Broccoli & Cheddar
Cheese, 102
Mushroom & Gruyère Tart with
Hazelnut Haricots Verts, 103
Oven Ribs with Mop Sauce &
Pecorino-Jalapeño-Dusted Corn, 38
Pork Chops with Apricots, Red
Cabbage & Blue Cheese, 46
Portobello Mushroom Parmesan with
Herbed Summer Squash, 96
Roasted Corn, Asparagus & Spring
Onion Salad with Fresh
Mozzarella, 95
Roasted Red Pepper, Spinach
& Asiago Stuffed Flank Steak with
Brown Sugared Carrots, 37
Stuffed Eggplant Three Ways, 90–91
Vegetable Pizza Tarts, 105
White Pizza with Potatoes &
Sun-Dried Tomatoes, 87

Chermoula, Roasted Tomato, 49

Chicken
Chicken Drumsticks with Green Olives
& Cipollini Onions, 27
Chicken Schnitzel with Asparagus, 28
Chicken Shawarma with Onions,
Peppers & Tahini Sauce, 24
Chicken Tikka Masala with Roasted
Cauliflower & Red Onion, 25
Dijon-Rosemary Chicken Thighs with
Maple-Glazed Pumpkin, 22
Roasted Chicken with Giant Croutons,
Sweet Potatoes & Arugula, 21
Spicy Asian Chicken Drumettes with
Broccoli & Spiced Walnuts, 30

Chimichurri Sauce, 70

Clams, Chorizo & Shrimp, Oven Paella
with, 73

Cod in Parchment with Tomatoes,
Olives & Spinach, 79

Corn
    Oven Ribs with Mop Sauce
        & Pecorino-Jalapeño-Dusted
        Corn, 38
    Roasted Corn, Asparagus & Spring
        Onion Salad with Fresh
        Mozzarella, 95
Cornbread-Sausage Stuffing & Kale,
    Turkey Roulade with, 29
Cucumber Raita, 57

D

Dates, Warm, & Wilted Arugula,
    Porchetta with, 51
Dijon-Rosemary Chicken Thighs with
    Maple-Glazed Pumpkin, 22

E

Eggplant
    Gingery Asian Eggplant with
        Tofu & Green Beans, 97
    Herb-Crusted Beef Tenderloin with
        Ratatouille, 43
    Lemony Tofu & Vegetable Kebabs
        with Roasted Poblano Sauce, 98
    Stuffed Eggplant Three Ways, 90–91
    Vietnamese Turkey Meatball
        & Hoisin Eggplant Banh Mi, 34
Eggs, Baked, Brussels Sprouts
    & Potato Hash with, 101
Empanadas, Pork & Green Chile,
    with Broccoli Rabe, 55

F

Fennel
    Roasted Mussels with Tomatoes,
        Fennel & Buttery Bread Crumbs, 68
    Whole Roasted Fish with Fennel,
        Lemons & Chimichurri Sauce, 70
Fish
    Ahi Tuna Niçoise Salad with
        Olive Oil–Dill Aioli, 65
    Cauliflower Steaks with Capers,
        Anchovies & Winter Greens, 92
    Cod in Parchment with Tomatoes,
        Olives & Spinach, 79

Creole Blackened Fish with
    Herbed Rice & Peas, 80
Miso-Glazed Mahimahi with
    Sesame-Sugar Snap Peas, 77
Roasted Caesar Salad with
    Salmon, 76
Salmon Provençal with Fingerling
    Potatoes & Cherry Tomatoes, 74
Whole Roasted Fish with Fennel,
    Lemons & Chimichurri Sauce, 70

G

Garlicky Shrimp with Asparagus Fries
    & Meyer Lemon Aioli, 66
Gingery Asian Eggplant with
    Tofu & Green Beans, 97
Grains. See also Rice
Stuffed Eggplant Three Ways, 90–91
Greens. See also Arugula; Kale; Spinach
    Cauliflower Steaks with Capers,
        Anchovies & Winter Greens, 92
    Roasted Caesar Salad with Salmon, 76

H

Herbs
    Chimichurri Sauce, 70
    Herb-Crusted Beef Tenderloin
        with Ratatouille, 43
    Roasted Tomato Chermoula, 49
Horseradish Sauce, 45

K

Kale
    Cauliflower Steaks with Capers,
        Anchovies & Winter Greens, 92
    Stuffed Eggplant Three Ways, 90–91
    Turkey Roulade with Sausage-
        Cornbread Stuffing & Kale, 29

L

Lamb
    Bruschetta with Chili-Spiced
        Leg of Lamb & Caramelized
        Red Onions, 58
    Moroccan-Spiced Lamb Chops
        with Vegetable Kebabs
        & Cucumber Raita, 57

Persian Stuffed Acorn Squash with
    Ground Lamb & Pomegranate, 52
Spiced Lamb Patties with
    Orange-Thyme Tapenade
    & Baby Artichokes, 54
Lemon, Meyer, Aioli, 66

M

Mahimahi, Miso-Glazed, with
    Sesame-Sugar Snap Peas, 77
Meat Loaf with Roasted Mushrooms
    & Smashed Butternut
    Squash, 35
Meyer Lemon Aioli, 66
Miso-Glazed Mahimahi with
    Sesame-Sugar Snap Peas, 77
Mushrooms
    Meat Loaf with Roasted
        Mushrooms & Smashed
        Butternut Squash, 35
    Mushroom & Gruyère Tart with
        Hazelnut Haricots Verts, 103
    Portobello Mushroom Parmesan
        with Herbed Summer Squash, 96
    Vegetable Pizza Tarts, 105
Mussels, Roasted, with Tomatoes,
    Fennel & Buttery Bread Crumbs, 68

O

Olives
    Ahi Tuna Niçoise Salad with
        Olive Oil–Dill Aioli, 65
    Chicken Drumsticks with Green Olives
        & Cipollini Onions, 27
    Cod in Parchment with Tomatoes,
        Olives & Spinach, 79
    Orange-Thyme Tapenade, 54
Onions
    Bruschetta with Chili-Spiced
        Leg of Lamb & Caramelized
        Red Onions, 58
    Chicken Drumsticks with Green Olives
        & Cipollini Onions, 27
    Chicken Shawarma with Onions,
        Peppers & Tahini Sauce, 24
    Chicken Tikka Masala with Roasted
        Cauliflower & Red Onion, 25

P

Paella, Oven, with Chorizo, Clams
& Shrimp, 73
Pancetta, Broccoli & Cheddar Cheese,
Loaded Baked Potatoes with, 102
Paprika-Yogurt Sauce, 25
Peas
Creole Blackened Fish with
Herbed Rice & Peas, 80
Miso-Glazed Mahimahi with
Sesame–Sugar Snap Peas, 77
Peppers
Chicken Shawarma with Onions,
Peppers & Tahini Sauce, 24
Mexican Stuffed Peppers with
Chipotle Sweet Potatoes, 33
Moroccan-Spiced Lamb Chops with
Vegetable Kebabs & Cucumber
Raita, 57
Oven Paella with Chorizo,
Clams & Shrimp, 73
Roasted Poblano Sauce, 98
Roasted Red Pepper, Spinach
& Asiago Stuffed Flank Steak with
Brown Sugared Carrots, 37
Skirt Steak with Smoky Compound
Butter & Blistered Shishito
Peppers, 44
Vegetable Pizza Tarts, 105
Pizza, White, with Potatoes
& Sun-Dried Tomatoes, 87
Pomegranate & Ground Lamb, Persian
Stuffed Acorn Squash with, 52
Pork. *See also* Sausages
Asian Five-Spice Pork Tenderloin with
Honey-Roasted Edamame, 48
Bangers & Smashed Potatoes with
Whole-Grain Dijonnaise, 40
Porchetta with Wilted Arugula
& Warm Dates, 51
Pork Chops with Apricots, Red
Cabbage & Blue Cheese, 46
Pork & Green Chile Empanadas
with Broccoli Rabe, 55
Pork Shoulder with Brussels Sprouts
& Roasted Tomato Chermoula, 49

Turkey Roulade with Sausage-
Cornbread Stuffing & Kale, 29
Zucchini Bolognese al Forno, 41
Portobello Mushroom Parmesan with
Herbed Summer Squash, 96
Potatoes. *See also* Sweet potatoes
Ahi Tuna Niçoise Salad with
Olive Oil–Dill Aioli, 67
Bangers & Smashed Potatoes with
Whole-Grain Dijonnaise, 40
Brussels Sprouts & Potato Hash
with Baked Eggs, 101
Loaded Baked Potatoes with Pancetta,
Broccoli & Cheddar Cheese, 102
Salmon Provençal with Fingerlings
& Cherry Tomatoes, 74
White Pizza with Potatoes &
Sun-Dried Tomatoes, 87
Pumpkin, Maple-Glazed, Dijon-
Rosemary Chicken Thighs with, 22

R

Rice
Creole Blackened Fish with
Herbed Rice & Peas, 80
Oven Paella with Chorizo,
Clams & Shrimp, 73

S

Salads
Ahi Tuna Niçoise Salad with
Olive Oil–Dill Aioli, 67
Roasted Caesar Salad with
Salmon, 76
Roasted Corn, Asparagus & Spring
Onion Salad with Mozzarella, 95
Salmon
Roasted Caesar Salad with
Salmon, 76
Salmon Provençal with Fingerlings
& Cherry Tomatoes, 74
Sauces
Chimichurri Sauce, 70
Cucumber Raita, 57
Horseradish Sauce, 45
Meyer Lemon Aioli, 64

Olive Oil–Dill Aioli, 67
Paprika-Yogurt Sauce, 25
Roasted Poblano Sauce, 98
Roasted Tomato Chermoula, 49
Tahini Sauce, 24
Sausages
Bangers & Smashed Potatoes with
Whole-Grain Dijonnaise, 40
Oven Paella with Chorizo, Clams
& Shrimp, 73
Turkey Roulade with Sausage-
Cornbread Stuffing & Kale, 29
Scallops, Roasted, with Spinach
& Lemons, 69
Shellfish
Garlicky Shrimp with Asparagus
Fries & Meyer Lemon Aioli, 66
Oven Paella with Chorizo, Clams
& Shrimp, 73
Roasted Mussels with Tomatoes,
Fennel & Buttery Bread Crumbs, 68
Roasted Scallops with Spinach
& Lemons, 69
Shrimp
Garlicky Shrimp with Asparagus Fries
& Meyer Lemon Aioli, 66
Oven Paella with Chorizo, Clams
& Shrimp, 73
Spinach
Cod in Parchment with Tomatoes,
Olives & Spinach, 79
Roasted Red Pepper, Spinach
& Asiago Stuffed Flank Steak with
Brown Sugared Carrots, 37
Roasted Scallops with Spinach
& Lemons, 69
Squash. *See also* Zucchini
Dijon-Rosemary Chicken Thighs with
Maple-Glazed Pumpkin, 22
Herb-Crusted Beef Tenderloin with
Ratatouille, 43
Meat Loaf with Roasted Mushrooms
& Smashed Butternut Squash, 35
Moroccan-Spiced Lamb Chops
with Vegetable Kebabs
& Cucumber Raita, 57

Persian Stuffed Acorn Squash
    with Ground Lamb
        & Pomegranate, 52
Portobello Mushroom Parmesan
    with Herbed Summer Squash, 96
Sweet potatoes
    Mexican Stuffed Peppers with
        Chipotle Sweet Potatoes, 33
    Roasted Chicken with Giant Croutons,
        Sweet Potatoes & Arugula, 21
    Standing Rib Roast with Rosemary
        Root Vegetables & Horseradish
            Sauce, 45

T
Tahini Sauce, 24
Tapenade, Orange-Thyme, 54
Tarts
    Mushroom & Gruyère Tart with
        Hazelnut Haricots Verts, 103
    Vegetable Pizza Tarts, 105
Tofu
    Gingery Asian Eggplant with
        Tofu & Green Beans, 97
    Lemony Tofu & Vegetable Kebabs
        with Roasted Poblano Sauce, 98
Tomatoes
    Ahi Tuna Niçoise Salad with
        Olive Oil–Dill Aioli, 67
    Cod in Parchment with Tomatoes,
        Olives & Spinach, 79
    Herb-Crusted Beef Tenderloin with
        Ratatouille, 43
    Roasted Mussels with Tomatoes,
        Fennel & Buttery Bread Crumbs, 68
    Roasted Tomato Chermoula, 49
    Salmon Provençal with Fingerling
        Potatoes & Cherry Tomatoes, 74
    Stuffed Eggplant Three Ways, 90–91
    White Pizza with Potatoes &
        Sun-Dried Tomatoes, 87
Turkey
    Turkey Roulade with Sausage-
        Cornbread Stuffing & Kale, 29
    Vietnamese Turkey Meatball
        & Hoisin Eggplant Banh Mi, 34

V
Vegetables. *See also specific vegetables*
    Standing Rib Roast with Rosemary
        Root Vegetables & Horseradish
            Sauce, 45
    Vegetable Pizza Tarts, 105
Vietnamese Turkey Meatball & Hoisin
    Eggplant Banh Mi, 34

W
Walnuts, Spiced, & Broccoli, Spicy
    Asian Chicken Drumettes with, 30

Y
Yogurt
    Cucumber Raita, 57
    Paprika-Yogurt Sauce, 25
    Stuffed Eggplant Three Ways, 90–91

Z
Zucchini
    Herb-Crusted Beef Tenderloin
        with Ratatouille, 43
    Lemony Tofu & Vegetable Kebabs
        with Roasted Poblano Sauce, 98
    Moroccan-Spiced Lamb Chops
        with Vegetable Kebabs
            & Cucumber Raita, 57
    Portobello Mushroom Parmesan
        with Herbed Summer Squash, 96
    Zucchini Bolognese al Forno, 41

SHEET PAN

Conceived and produced by Weldon Owen, Inc.

Weldon Owen is a division of Bonnier Publishing USA

A WELDON OWEN PRODUCTION

1045 Sansome Street, Suite 100
San Francisco, CA 94111
www.weldonowen.com

Printed and bound in the China

First printed in 2016
10 9 8 7 6 5 4 3

Library of Congress Cataloging-in-Publication
data is available.

ISBN 13: 978-1-68188-137-9
ISBN 10: 1-68188-137-3

WELDON OWEN, INC.

President & Publisher Roger Shaw
SVP, Sales & Marketing Amy Kaneko
Finance & Operations Director Philip Paulick

Associate Publisher Amy Marr
Project Editor Lesley Bruynesteyn

Creative Director Kelly Booth
Art Director Marisa Kwek
Senior Production Designer Rachel Lopez Metzger

Production Director Chris Hemesath
Associate Production Director Michelle Duggan
Imaging Manager Don Hill

Photographer Ray Kachatorian
Food Stylist Valerie Aikman-Smith
Prop Stylist Gena Sigala

ACKNOWLEDGMENTS

Weldon Owen wishes to thank the following people for their generous support in
producing this book: Dennis Ayuson, Kris Balloun, Kim Byrne, Amanda Frederickson,
Rachel Markowitz, Alexis Mersel, Carolyn Miller, Elizabeth Parson,
Michelle Reinerlight, Alyse Sakai, and Tuan Tran.